SILICON MINDS

THE SCIENCE, IMPACT, AND PROMISE OF ARTIFICIAL INTELLIGENCE

THIEN-NAM DINH

International Rights

If you are interested in purchasing the international or foreign language rights to this book, please email: contact@wisefoxpub.com

Errors and Feedback
Please Contact Us If You Find Any Errors

While every effort is taken to ensure the quality and accuracy of this book, spelling, grammar and other errors are often missed in the early versions of publication.

We appreciate you contacting us first if you noticed any errors in this book before taking any other action.

If you find any issues or errors with this book, please contact us and we'll correct these as soon as possible.

Readers that notify us of errors will be invited to receive advance reader copies of future books published.

Errors: errors@wisefoxpub.com

Feedback

For any general feedback about the book, please feel free to contact us at the email address below:

Feedback: feedback@wisefoxpub.com

CONTENTS

BONUS AI RESOURCES GUIDE

Get the bonus Artificial Intelligence Study guide.

At the back of this book are answers to the questions in the chapters along with further learning resources.

You can also get a free copy of these in PDF format for easier access.

The guide includes Appendix A and B in PDF format with resources to learn more about A.I, Machine Learning and NLP.

The resource guide also includes a quick reference guide of all the questions and answers included at the end of each chapter of this book.

Start learning A.I and master the future of technology.

Visit the website below to get your copy:
www.wisefoxbooks.com/aiguide

REVIEWS AND FEEDBACK

Reviews

If you enjoy this book, it would be greatly appreciated if you were able to take a few moments to share your opinion and post a review on Amazon after you finish reading it.

Even a few words and a rating can be a great help.

Feedback

If you don't enjoy the book or have any feedback, please let us know what you didn't enjoy by emailing feedback@wisefoxpub.com

We welcome all comments as they help improve the book based on your feedback.

ABOUT THE AUTHOR

Thien-Nam Dinh is a professional computer scientist working at Sandia National Laboratories, a prominent center for research and technological development in the Southwestern United States.

Thien-Nam earned a Bachelor in Engineering from the University of Delaware, graduating summa cum laude. Before completing his undergraduate studies, Thien-Nam shifted his focus to computer science in order to prepare for a transition to the field for further education. He subsequently attended Rice University through Sandia's Master's Fellowship program where he earned a Master's degree in Computer Science. His work currently includes research and development with machine learning and blockchain technology, among other exciting projects.

Thien-Nam was first exposed to ideas about AI by his high school physics teacher, and it has since shaped everything from his profession career to his interests and political views. His hobbies include reading, exploring, and letting people know that his opinions do not reflect those of Sandia, NTESS, or the United States federal government.[1]

His professional and academic background - combined with a lifelong passion for reading and creative writing - gives

Thien-Nam a uniquely engaging writing style that will help you learn a lot about AI and enjoy it every step of the way.

About the Editor

Daniel Frumkin is a professional writer specializing in copywriting and technical writing in the cryptocurrency industry. He is the author of *Understanding Blockchain: Learn How Blockchain Technology is Powering Bitcoin, Cryptocurrencies, and the Future of the Internet*, and also writes for Invest in Blockchain, a rapidly growing cryptocurrency media platform geared toward educated investors.

Daniel earned a B.Sc. in Mechanical Engineering from the University of New Mexico. He chose to work as a writer rather than an engineer in order to achieve location independence, which he has since utilized to travel extensively and to live for short times in China and multiple locations around Europe.

Prior to working on Silicon Minds, Daniel had limited exposure to AI. It has now become one of his strongest interests, and his new knowledge has helped him to identify some of the countless cryptocurrency projects that use AI to generate hype without adequate justification.

1. The views expressed in this book do not necessarily represent the views of Sandia National Laboratories, NTESS, the U.S. Department of Energy or the United States Government.

About The Editor

Daniel Frumkin is a professional writer specializing in copywriting and technical writing in the cryptocurrency industry. He is the author of *Understanding Blockchain: Learn How Blockchain Technology is Powering Bitcoin, Cryptocurrencies, and the Future of the Internet*, and also writes for Invest in Blockchain, a rapidly growing cryptocurrency media platform geared toward educated investors.

Daniel earned a B.Sc. in Mechanical Engineering from the University of New Mexico. He chose to work as a writer rather than an engineer in order to achieve location independence, which he has since utilized to travel extensively and to live for short times in China and multiple locations around Europe.

Prior to working on Silicon Minds, Daniel had limited exposure to AI. It has now become one of his strongest interests, and his new knowledge has helped him to identify some of the countless cryptocurrency projects that use AI to generate hype without adequate justification.

---

1. *The views expressed in this book do not necessarily represent the views of Sandia National Laboratories, NTESS, the U.S. Department of Energy or the United States Government.*

FOREWARD

For the curious mind, there is perhaps no more intriguing a subject than artificial intelligence in the early 21st century. There are so many big questions to ponder: Will AI bring about the end for humanity? Or will it usher in a new age of unparalleled human prosperity for generations to come? Will AI ever become conscious, and if so, how will we even be able to tell? On a more personal note, will I still be able to find a job in 10-15 years? Will I even need to?

I consider myself lucky to have even begun pondering these questions. And I have my friendship with Thien-Nam to thank for that, as it was his interest in AI that eventually piqued my own.

The first time Thien-Nam and I ever talked about AI is still a vivid memory in my mind. We were both entering the final few semesters of our undergraduate studies in university, both studying mechanical engineering. If I'm being honest, I had chosen the major because I was truly clueless as to what I wanted to do with my life when I was 18, so copying

Thien-Nam's decision seemed like my safest bet. And so it came as quite a shock to me when Thien-Nam told me that engineering was not the best path for him after all, and he was changing course in order to enter the field of computer science.

I wondered, *what could possibly be interesting enough about computers that he would do this so close to graduation?* The answer was AI. "The things we're are working on now are pretty incredible" he told me, "but in the long run, can it ever compare to AI? It's what comes afterwards that I hope we'll be around to see."

In the years since then, I learned a little bit about AI here and there. HBO's *Westworld* even provided some great stimulation for thinking further about some of those big questions I mentioned in the first paragraph. But it wasn't until I read this book that I truly understood why Thien-Nam had changed paths years ago.

Silicon Minds reads nothing like a dry textbook or an overly dumbed-down *AI for Beginners* guidebook. Rather, it is a deeply engaging and thought-provoking storybook that helped me to understand both the technical and the philosophical sides to AI. Moreover, it gave me a framework with which to think about those big AI questions more clearly and rationally.

I wouldn't recommend this book for everybody. For those who don't know much about AI yet, like me before I read it, you can expect to be challenged and to think critically throughout the reading process. If you're looking for an easy read, this book may not be for you.

With that being said, for the intellectually curious individual who is ready to dip their toes into this exciting field, I can't recommend Silicon Minds enough. Pushing through the challenging early chapters about the technical side of AI is well worth the reward of exploring the field's future possibilities with that technical foundation in the latter chapters. But be warned... Once you start learning and thinking about AI, you might never want to stop.

INTRODUCTION

"Artificial intelligence is the future, not only for Russia, but for all of humankind. It comes with colossal opportunities, but also threats that are difficult to predict. Whoever becomes the leader in this sphere will become the ruler of the world."
  - Vladmir Putin

I t's a typical Sunday morning. You're at home, sipping on your favorite Sunday beverage when suddenly, new and alarming headlines flash across your news feed.

Neural network learns to predict summer musical hits

An artificial intelligence developed its own non-human language

Alexa learns to love; secret wedding planned with Siri!

What do you do? Well, if your name is Elon Musk, then you

frantically search your couch cushion for spare change, schedule a press conference, and announce your new multi-billion dollar investment to fight the impending AI invasion.

If your name isn't Elon Musk, then maybe the recent news has peaked your interest enough to look more into all of this fuss. That probably led you to picking up a new book. This book. If so, you've come to the right place! In the subsequent chapters, we will be exploring all of the important aspects of artificial intelligence with a high-level, introductory approach. For now, let's first get our feet wet with some initial discussion.

Why You Should Care

First things first: why should you even care? Why AI instead of genetic engineering or nanotechnology? Why crazy futuristic technologies at all rather than tax codes or gardening tips? The short answer is that AI is important. What used to be only relevant to computer researchers and wayward philosophy majors is now a topic that needs to be understood by everyone.

Already, AI has infiltrated every corner of our lives. Every time you interact with a smart device or an internet service, you are most likely triggering an AI program. Behind the scenes, algorithms work tirelessly to make just about everything a little cheaper, a little safer, and a little more personalized. As we move forward, what we call AI today will only be a tip of the iceberg.

It's unlikely that getting familiar with AI will help you pay the bills any time soon. But this book, and the field in general, is about thinking for the long term. Maybe you'll one day find yourself in the middle of a totally overturned job market. Maybe you'll soon tune in to discover a new wave of tech-driven political upheavals. In exponential times, flexibility and knowledge is the most valuable currency. As we transition into this new world, no technology, no movement, no product of the human mind will carry as much weight as artificial intelligence.

Defining AI

So what is AI, exactly? It turns out that this is a fairly complicated question and will be discussed in more detail in Chapter 2. However, here is a small taste:

Artificial Intelligence is the ability of a man-made system to replicate human thoughts

This seems like a straightforward definition. That is, until you remember that no such thing really exists. Sure, The Terminator, R2-D2, and WALL-E all seem to have some type of artificial intelligence, but when was the last time you met a thinking machine in person? We're simply not there yet. And so, to justify all of the headlines that you've recently read, we need a much more conservative definition:

Artificial Intelligence is the ability to solve hard perception and decision-making problems with advanced algorithms.

By perception, we mean tasks like recognizing cat pictures and english words. By decision-making, we mean choices like how to delete email spam. This is a somewhat less exciting definition, but it's a start. As you will see, "hard problems" and "advanced algorithms" are very loose definitions that are constantly changing with what we consider to be "hard" and "advanced". This is an unfortunate characteristic of the field.

Hopefully, the technology will eventually get to a point where we can phase out this second definition in favor of the first one. As of the writing of this book, today is not that day.

A Short History

The concept of AI has been around for a very, very long time. Amazingly, some of the first mentions of "mechanical robots" and "artificial beings" can be found in early Greek Mythology. They imagined life-like moving statues and giant mechanical automata who patrolled the oceans hunting for pirates and invaders. However, for those of us born on this side of the Trojan War, AI is inseparable from our beloved digital computers. As a result, modern AI can be considered a subfield of computer science, one with a rich and volatile history.

The Early Days (1950-1974): The modern idea of AI was formally introduced by Alan Turing, British war hero, star subject of *The Imitation Game (2014)*, and widely accepted "father of computer science". In those days, much of the work was in logic and mathematics. Moving around and looking at things seemed easy; even monkeys could do that. They believed the essence of what it meant to be intelligent is the ability to do algebra and geometry. Beginning with the Dartmouth Conference organized by another famous scientist named John McCarthy, researchers devoted most of their time toward solving these tasks. The milestones were crushed in spectacular fashion and true, human-like AI was presumed to be mere decades away.

The First AI Winter (1974-1980): True, human-like AI was not mere decades away. As it turns out, there is more to life than being really, really, really ridiculously good at math. Research funding dried up, and the field came grinding to a halt.

Resurgence (1980-1987): After much consideration, researchers realized that *knowledge* was a key component to intelligence. Scientists developed sophisticated methods to build useful knowledge databases. This information was reinforced by input from human experts in various fields and the resulting technology turned out to be incredibly useful for businesses. Funding reemerged, and true, human-like AI was presumed to be mere decades away.

The Second AI Winter (1987-1993): True, human-like AI was not mere decades away. Once again, funding dried up and research came grinding to a halt.

. . .

Big Computation (1993-2011): Since the first resurgence, the speed and power of computers had been growing exponentially. In this second resurgence, engineers created much more advanced algorithms which leveraged these supercomputers for solving problems in many specialized fields. Perhaps the most dramatic event occurred in 1997 when Microsoft's Deep Blue AI became the first computer program to defeat the reigning world chess champion. At long last, true, human-like AI was presumed to be mere decades... wait.

Current State

Today, AI benefits from the previous successes and failures of its eventful history. On top of the logical framework, knowledge-based systems, and computationally powerful algorithms discovered in the past, we now have access to vast amounts of data that would absolutely amaze Alan Turing and his contemporaries.

With the help of these tools, academic, government, and private organizations have collaborated to engineer a seemingly infinite variety of AI systems that touches every corner of society. To list just a few of these: autocorrect, personal digital assistants like Siri, high-frequency stock trading, self-driving cars, search engines, and targeted advertising are all examples of the growing number of applications. In this book, we'll cover many of these subjects as well as the technical buzzwords that you often see associated with them, things like "deep learning", "robotics", and "natural language processing".

Perhaps it's no surprise given the reliance on personal data that AI has trended toward becoming more and more human-centric. This means that progress has moved on from the impersonal mathematical realms of the 1950s to areas that more disturbingly encroach on our personal space and privacy. Although this gets us closer to the ultimate goal of AI, it also poses many concerns for ethics and policies along the way.

More so than any other technical field, AI is a deeply philosophical and existential topic. It's the subject of borderline religious eagerness for some and dramatic doomsday predictions for others. However, with all due respect to many extremely accomplished individuals, it does appear to be the case that many of the most provocative statements about AI originate with people who do not actually work within the field.

So the next time that you feel overwhelmed, remember the lessons of the first two AI winters. In a few decades, true, human-like AI will probably still be decades away. A third winter may still be coming. Here in 2018, however, the field is now entering a bona fide golden summer of progress.

Roadmap

We'll be covering a lot of topics in the following chapters. Although massive bodies of literature have been written in the past about very specialized aspects, the purpose of this book is to offer a broad, concise, and hopefully, more engaging look into the AI phenomena. Here is a sneak peak into what this will look like:

- Chapters 2-4: In these slightly more technical chapters, we will lay some of the core groundwork for understanding the definition of

AI, the various types, and the techniques used to power them.

- Chapters 5-6: We will proceed to discuss concrete applications of AI in everyday life and business to better understand its already tremendous impact in the world.
- Chapters 7-9: Finally, we'll end with the near-term future trends, its social consequences, and the fantastical world of possibilities that is yet to come.

You were born too late to explore the world and born too early to explore the galaxy. However, with a little luck, you'll be around just in time to appreciate the rise of the most significant creation ever conceived by humankind. We'd better get started.

Reflections

At the end of every chapter, I will pose some questions for self-reflection. If you have trouble with some of them, then don't worry! The questions are supposed to be a little challenging and most of them don't have right answers. Try your best, and if you need some inspiration, then an appendix of suggested answers is given at the end of the book.

1. Based on the second, weaker definition of AI, what are some examples of computer programs that we should *not* consider to be AI?
2. What might make problems like self-driving cars

and speech recognition so much harder than math problems?

3. If Big Data is the most important development in this era of AI research, what do you think will be the next big development?

WHAT IS AI?

"We are not interested in the fact that the brain has the consistency of cold porridge.

We don't want to say 'This machine's quite hard, so it isn't a brain, so it can't think.' "

- Alan Turing

In the first chapter, I said that an exact definition for AI would be somewhat tricky to pin down. I also hinted at the fact that there are two layers to look at it: one that encompasses the final, ultimate goal of AI, and one that applies to the more limited version which we see today. The first type is often referred to as *strong* or *general* AI while the second type is referred to as *weak* or *narrow* AI. In this chapter, we will explore the terms in greater detail and learn how to recognize them in the real world.

Strong AI

Strong AI refers to an AI with general intelligence that is capable of doing just about everything that humans can do.

Nothing close exist today and as a result, the study of strong AI is mostly left to philosophers and science fiction writers. But strong AI will arrive someday. When that day comes, will it be possible to recognize them? The answer is "maybe".

AI in Hollywood are most often portrayed as realistic, natural, and conspicuously attractive humanoids. However, when Alan Turing first described thinking computers in 1950, he had the foresight to understand that a test for true artificial intelligence should not be limited by the ability to look and feel human. In his view, it is not our fleshy organic brains that define our intelligence, but the ability to act with our rational, thinking minds. In a simple thought experiment, he invented what would become known as the famous *Turing Test* for intelligence:

A human tester, let's call her Alice, chats with two unknown parties through a messaging app. One participant is a human and the other is a computer program that tries to act like a human. After some long period of time, Alice attempts to guess which party is which. If she cannot do so at a success rate that is much higher than pure chance, then the computer program has fooled her. It has passed the Turing Test for true intelligence.

To this day, the Turing Test remains the most influential thought experiment governing the philosophy of AI. It neatly side-steps tricky concepts like "consciousness" and "souls". The only thing that matters, in the Turing Test, is intelligent behavior.

Unfortunately, it also has its drawbacks. Namely, the test itself is very biased toward human-like intelligence. Who is to say that there are not strongly intelligent systems that can think as well or better than us without needing to mimic our unnecessary quirks? As a result, what we can say is that while the Turing Test might be a *sufficient* test for intelligence, it is not a *necessary* test. In other words, if a machine passes the test then it's probably intelligent. However, if it fails, then we can't say for certain that it's *not* intelligent.

To make this point more clear, suppose that computers finally take over the world and it becomes necessary for us humans to prove our own intelligence in a *Reverse Turing Test*. Here is how that might go:

> *AI Tester: Human, what's the square root of 42?*
> *Human Subject: .... Bleep bloop blop....*

And just like that, the human subject has failed. Hopefully our machine overlords will discover a better way to characterize intelligence. For now, the Turing Test seems to be the best that we have.

Weak AI

The AI that exists today are called weak, or narrow AI. While they can be impressive in their own right, they are really only adept at performing very specific tasks. A definition here is slightly more tricky.

To get started, first imagine that we have a list containing things that we generally want to call AI, things like spam detection, chatbots, and self-driving cars. Next, imagine that we have a different list containing things that we do not want to call AI, things like email servers, trains, and vending machines. The challenge now is to identify a few key properties that logically distinguishes the two lists. Here are is a first attempt at identifying just two characteristics:

Rule 1: It performs a task that humans would do anyways if computers couldn't

Rule 2: The task involves a multi-step mental calculation

Let's see how these rules apply to some sample machine operations:

	Rule 1	Rule 2
Drive a car	yes	yes
Route internet packets	no	yes
Recognize cat pictures	yes	yes
Trade stocks	yes	yes
Toast bread	yes	no
Copy a pdf	no	no

So far, so good. These two simple rules seem to do a reasonable job of singling out the tasks that most humans would call AI: self-driving cars, image recognition, and stock trading. But wait, let's now take a look at some slightly more problematic counter examples:

	Rule 1	Rule 2
Multiply two numbers	yes	yes
Balance a checkbook	yes	yes
Encrypt a message	yes	yes

What gives? Are we saying that calculators and spreadsheets use AI as well? The first two rules would say yes. However, intuitively, these last few examples don't seem like they should be grouped with self-driving cars and stock trading.

These tasks are too *easy*. And so, as a second attempt, we'll add another rule:

The task has to be hard.

With that, we now have a final loose definition for weak AI. It's pretty subjective but unfortunately, it's the best we can do.

This is the major problem with defining weak AI. How do you define a hard task when everything seems to get easier as technology advances? People alive in 1642, when the first mechanical calculator was created, must have considered the achievement to be every bit as remarkable as the advances in "AI" that we see today. Four hundred years from now, I have no doubt that our state-of-the-art technology will seem completely mundane. A definition for weak AI has and always will be a moving target. As computer scientist Larry Tesler once bitterly stated:

AI is whatever hasn't been done yet

Hard Problems

There will never be a perfect definition that stands the test of time. What we can do, at least, is try to explain the difficulty of the problems that modern AI tries to solve. In this way, you'll be well-equipped to appreciate the amazing research that has recently emerged and perhaps even anticipate the next wave of advances.

Loosely speaking, "hardness" comes in two flavors: size and complexity. To be considered hard, a problem needs to be challenging in both respects.

Large Problems

Let's start with size. In a typical weak AI application, there is a well-stated problem and some unknown solutions. The job of the AI program is to find the best solution that it can. One way to measure the "size" of an AI problem is to look at the number of possible solutions, no matter if it is right or wrong. The collection of possible solutions is called the problem's *search space*. Here is a simple concrete example:

Problem: Win a game of tic-tac-toe
Solutions: A list of the best moves to make for any given situation

In this case, the size of the search space is related to the number of possible game situations on the tic-tac-toe board, which we call states. Every legal combination of X's and O's that can occur in a real game is its own unique state.

If you list out all of the possible scenarios, then it turns out that there are exactly 5812. In computing terms, this is tiny. Playing tic-tac-toe does not require AI, just some very simple game theory and the computing power of a potato. Solving problems by listing out all of the possibilities is called a *brute force* approach because it doesn't require any sophisticated decision making.

For some perspective, chess is a much, much more complicated game. The number of possible states in chess is 10^{47}, close to the number of atoms on our planet and far more than we can ever hope to list out on Earth-based computers. This is why we still care about chess in the field of AI. Even though computers have left humans in the dust since 1997, The World Computer Chess Championship still crowns newer and better AI champions every year.

Even more impressive is the recent victory of Google's AlphaGo program in a popular Chinese board game called Go. The search space in Go depends on a truly mind-boggling 10^{170} possible states. To even attempt to understand this number, first take the observable universe. Now imagine that every single atom itself has a miniature universe spinning inside it. Take the total number of atoms in all the miniature universes, multiply it again by ten billion, and you'll finally have the number of possible states in Go. Even the word "astronomical" is itself astronomically lacking in its ability to describe this truly incomprehensible space.

AlphaGo's victory was a monumental achievement that shattered all expert predictions for AI progress. However, there are countless more fascinating problems in computer science that boast similar, or even larger search spaces. These are the mathematical playgrounds of weak AI, where researchers are constantly looking for newer and more efficient ways to find answers.

Complex Problems

Not all large problems are difficult, however. Here is an example of what appears to be a fairly easy problem.

> *Problem: Find the best answer to 58 x 18*
> *Solutions: All real numbers on the number line*

This is a very large problem by all accounts. After all, the number of potential solutions is... well, infinite. There are infinitely many numbers on the number line, and therefore an infinite number of wrong answers to wade through. Still, any grade school student could solve this problem. What gives?

While the search space is infinite, the process needed to explore it is exceedingly simple. We don't need to check every single point on the number line to see whether it might be the right answer. Instead, humans and computers alike employ some basic shortcuts to arrive at the solution in a handful of steps. The problem is not very *complex*.

Truly complex problems are nearly impossible to solve efficiently. One of the most famous and deceptively complex problems in computer science is called the traveling salesman problem. It can be stated as follows:

Bob is an insurance salesman who routinely travels for work. He sells AI software, of course. Every month, he gets a new list of potential clients who live in various parts of the country. Bob's wife has been pretty upset with how long he stays away from home, so his job is to visit every client on the list while doing the *least* amount of traveling that he possibly can.

Problem: Determine the shortest path that reaches every client
Solutions: A schedule specifying the order to visit them

Go ahead, try to solve it! What you want to find is a general-purpose solution, i.e. an algorithm, that will let Bob find the short path between any combination of possible locations. There's a small chance that some algorithm does exist, and maybe you'll be the one to find it. If so, then congratulations. Fame, fortune, and academic immortality are soon coming your way.

If not, then no need to worry. Although they haven't succeeded in proving it yet, most theoretical researchers are beginning to believe that no solution exists at all. This problem is what computer scientists call *np-complete*, where "np" stands for "nondeterministic polynomial time". Don't worry about the exact terminology, just imagine that it is a synonym for "very, very complicated."

How complicated? Well, a slightly more precise definition for np-completeness is that there are no strategies which are guaranteed to work much faster than a brute force approach. You can introduce as many clever steps as you want, and it wouldn't matter.

In this case, Bob would have to apply brute force to a search space that is just as massive as the ones we saw earlier in chess and Go. At 10 clients, there are about a thousand different routes that Bob needs to list and compare. At 40, there are a trillion. By only 270 clients, he's back to the number of atoms in the universe.

It is very important to realize that these problems are by

no means purely hypothetical. Delivery services like FedEx care a lot about the traveling salesman problem for obvious reasons. You may be more surprised to learn, however, that versions of this problem routinely pop up in circuit design, telecommunications, and social media analysis. The ubiquity of interrelated complex problems is precisely why AI is so important in our changing world.

How AI Works

By now, you should have a slightly better concept for the types of problems that AI tries to solve and why they are so difficult. Given these immense challenges, how does AI actually solve them? The name of the game is to more quickly find approximate solutions that are "good enough". Any route by the traveling salesman that will bring him home before his wife gets *too* angry is acceptable. We don't need a perfect chess program, just one that can best our puny human brains.

AI searches for these acceptable solutions with the help of *constraints* and *heuristics*.

Constraints - States that an AI should avoid at all costs. Examples are "be home for Christmas" for the traveling salesman or "don't drive on the sidewalk" for self-driving cars.

Heuristics - A set of guidelines that the AI uses to try to make the best decisions at any given time. You can think of them as mental shortcuts. For instance, spam filters might do a quick search for the number of times "SALE" or "CHEAP VIAGRA!!!" shows up.

By definition, heuristics will never be 100% perfect. Sure, most spam is pretty obvious, but maybe you really do have that one friend who gets oddly excited about cheap Viagra sales. The moment we find a perfect heuristic, the problem is no longer interesting. True AI is therefore doomed to navigate an immensely complicated world with nothing more than imperfect shortcuts and rough approximations for how it should act. Incidentally, this isn't so different from the way that you and I wander through this figuratively np-complete problem that we call "life".

Defining AI is just the beginning, but it's a start. In this chapter, we've covered a few concepts that will re-emerge time and time again in the more technical discussion of AI. These include:

- search space
- complexity
- constraints
- heuristics

Part of the art of working with AI deals with choosing the right constraints and heuristics to solve these profoundly hard problems. As we shall see in later chapters, heuristics might be pre-programmed by coders and human experts. Or, in the case of machine learning, they might be naturally discovered by specialized algorithms.

Actually, solving these problems, of course, is the real challenge. Before AI became the economic sensation that it is today, it was a purely technical field that captivated some of the most brilliant minds that the world has seen. It's still as challenging as ever. In the next chapter, we'll take the foundation that we've covered in this one to explore the incredible diversity of modern AI research.

Reflections

1. Can you think of any better alternatives to the Turing Test that will include *all* possible strong AI?
2. What are some heuristics that a chess-playing program might use to decide whether it is winning or losing? If you are not familiar with chess then feel free to pick your favorite strategy-based game.
3. In tic-tac-toe, we said that there were 5812 possible states, but the search space is actually a list of moves for any possible state. With that in mind, how big is the search space, roughly? How about for chess?

SECTORS OF AI

"Nobody phrases it this way, but I think that artificial intelligence is almost a humanities discipline. It's really an attempt to understand human intelligence and human cognition."

- Sebastian Thrun

AI is characterized by an almost maddeningly stubborn tendency to avoid categorization. On one hand, the overarching goal is fairly straight-forward: to replicate the cognitive functions of human-like intelligence. On the other hand, the fact that different fields within AI exist at all is clear evidence that we haven't quite "put it all together" yet. The addition of a seemingly endless variety of applications only adds to the confusion.

To keep things straight, I find it helpful to adopt Sebastian Thrun's philosophy. One great way is to maintain a mental map between fields of AI and our own cognitive functions.

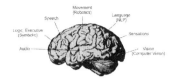

There is a pretty satisfying correspondence between major areas of ongoing research in AI and various functional areas of the brain as uncovered by neuroscience. Charting development in this way sometimes feels as if we're excavating the expanses of a giant digital brain that is slowly coming into existence. Maybe the right people will put it all together someday, but for now it's a classic tale of seven blind mice.

Robotics

Robots are a go-to for mental imagery when thinking about AI. Although they are mostly confined to industrial and military applications for now, there is no doubt that very real changes are coming to the world with the advent of drones, self-driving cars, and personal robots.

Robotics is an interdisciplinary field whose study includes the physics of moving machines (mechanical engineering) as well as the underlying sensors and circuitry (electrical engineering). From a computer science and AI perspective, robotics mostly entails the *planning* of movement: how to navigate a robot from point A to point B using whatever set of wheels and limbs it has at its disposal. In the simplest case, pretend we have a single point robot which can move anywhere in two dimensions on a fixed map. Its goal is to get from the start to finish without hitting obstacles along the way.

Any toddler can solve this problem by hand, but it's not at all obvious how best to encode the solution in a computer program. There are many different approaches, but one of best methods that scales well to larger and more complex problems is called *sample-based planning*. Here is how it works:

1. Randomly place points in free areas of the map
2. Connect each point with its closest neighbors, if possible
3. Find the shortest route through the points to reach the finish line

This navigation problem lies at the heart of robotics AI. Of course, the example shown above was only the simplest toy version of the problem. Things become much harder when we start to add constraints and uncertainty, which may include one or more of the following complications:

1. The sensors and motors are not perfect.
2. Pesky humans and other parts of the environment keep getting in the way.
3. The robot doesn't actually know where it is, and/or it doesn't have a complete map. Roboticists call this the SLAM problem (simultaneous localization and mapping).
4. The robot is moving so fast that we care about physical limits on speed and acceleration. This is where mechanical engineers come in.
5. There is more than one robot.

More generally, the problem also gets exponentially harder if the robot has many moving parts. I won't get into too much detail here because this is a pretty abstract subject, but the gist is that for each moving part, the planning happens *as if* we had added new dimensions to the map. This is because the robot needs a plan for every interconnected joint and motor. In our example problem, the point robot is navigating in two dimensions: up/down and left/right. A bare-bones humanoid robot must navigate through about two dozen dimensions.

Does that mean that AI researchers have learned how to

think in more than three dimensions? Nope, they're scientists, not wizards. It's very difficult to figure out distances and collision avoidance in this weird high-dimensional search space. That's where clever mathematical heuristics come in and why robotic motion planning is a stellar challenge for AI.

Computer Vision

Most people are familiar with how far computer graphics have come along over the years. Here in the United States, the science of turning computer code into cute animated animals and violent explosions sits at the forefront of a 10-billion-dollar film industry and 23-billion-dollar video game industry.

Computer vision deals with roughly the opposite problem: the science of turning human-generated images into a form that can be understood by computers. Any complicated robot such as a self-driving car will need some level of computer vision to move around. Many tech companies are also interested in this field for different applications like image searches and facial recognition.

In a computer vision problem, the program receives a digital image and outputs some type of *decision*. This is usually a small piece of information such as "is this a cat?" or "how many people are in this picture?". To your eyes, images are full of distinct features and meaning. To a computer, they are nothing more than grids of pixels represented by varying numbers. It can only come to "understand" the image by taking the following steps:

1. Pre-processing - Clean up the image for easier processing by intelligently reducing noise,

changing colors, or re-scaling parts of the picture.

2. Feature Extraction - Detect points of interest such as lines and corners. For instance, the existence of a line is inferred when two neighboring regions of pixels have clearly different values for color.

3. Detection - Locate relevant segments. Now that the program has some notion of the image's low-level features, it locates important objects like words and faces.

4. Decision making - Finally, the important objects are compared with a database of previously analyzed pictures to make a decision for the final output decision.

New challenges come to play when dealing with videos or using different angles of the same scene to reconstruct a 3D model. Another growing field of study is "one-shot learning", where algorithms attempt to say something interesting about the images without the need to maintain large databases of old examples.

The previous discussion on robotics should have given you some appreciation for the surprising difficulty in re-creating basic human movement that we take for granted every day. Vision is no different. The entire time you have been reading this book, your visual cortex has been furiously working to filter out details and fill in gaps in the complete picture that you *think* you have in your mind. Although 30-60% of your brain is devoted to this task, the whole process feels effortless. It's no wonder that researchers in the 1950s thought motion planning and computer vision would be solved in a matter of years.

Today, neuroscience gives us a better sense for the amazing complexity of our natural visual capabilities. We still have a long, long way to go in AI, and the finish line is nowhere in sight. Especially if you're a computer.

Natural Language Processing

Here in the early 21st century, most people owe their first encounters with AI to advances in natural language processing (NLP). Auto-completion, personal assistants like Siri and Cortana, Google translate, and those insanely annoying customer service call menus are all shining examples of the good and bad of NLP.

At its core, natural language processing is the study of how spoken human language can be analyzed and digested into a form that computers can understand. If we all spoke the way that computers do, NLP would hardly be an interesting problem.

Since we don't, it's up to AI researchers to navigate the hot mess of nouns, verbs, adjectives, adverbs, articles, prepositions, clauses, subclauses, conjugations, conjunctions, tenses, pronouns, abbreviations and acronyms that English-speaking humans use to communicate. Once AI can manage that, it still has to deal with the much hotter mess composed of slang, sarcasm, connotation, and context. Dealing with this second set of complications is a largely unsolved problem. Other languages obviously come with more challenges as well.

. . .

Researchers realized fairly early on that the job of hand-programming algorithms to account for the situational quirks of human language would be a pretty futile and thankless task. You probably struggle with the inaccuracies of NLP every day on your smartphone. As a result, NLP has been a predominantly statistical field of study since as early as the 1980s. Every result that comes from an NLP program is meaningless without an attached probability stating the likelihood of correctness.

One of the most dramatic events in AI history occurred when IBM's Watson defeated human champions in the popular trivia game of Jeopardy. If you haven't already, I'd encourage you to go and watch the video of this event. It's quite interesting to see how Watson assigns probabilities for each of his answers.

For most people watching Jeopardy, the challenge of the game is to remember obscure trivia facts. For Watson, the exact opposite is true. Facts are easy; it has access to the entire Internet. The challenge for Watson was only to understand the question in a way that would unlock humanity's vast store of digital knowledge. This is an extremely important concept that distinguishes NLP from other technologies, and why NLP has so much potential. It can be summed up in the following truism:

An AI that walks like a human is worth one human. An AI that talks like a human is worth 10 billion.

These days, Watson splits his time between answering medical inquiries, providing tutoring sessions, and more or less shouldering the hopes and dreams of IBM in the modern tech landscape. AI such as Watson and the growing host of other well-known personal assistants will only become increasingly pervasive in our everyday lives. Eventually, they will come to change not only how we interact with our devices, but how we think about the acquisition of knowledge itself.

Symbolic AI

The final broad area of AI research l want to mention is symbolic AI, sometimes referred to as GOFAI (Good Old-Fashioned AI). Symbolic AI deals with mathematical ideas in areas like logic, knowledge representation, and planning. It attempts to recreate intelligence by thinking in a formal way that humans or, more precisely, mathematicians and philosophers, might understand. Concepts understood by these AI are embedded in the software as human-readable symbols, hence the name.

The purest form of symbolic AI features a *knowledge base*, which encodes well-defined facts known to the AI, and an *inference engine*, which is used to introspectively discover new unknown facts. In the classic example, a simple AI has the following knowledge base:

All humans are mortal.

Socrates is a human.

From these facts, the AI should be able to apply its inference engine and make the following conclusion:

Socrates is mortal.

Mind-blowing, right? From this example alone, you might conclude that this symbolic AI business is not very useful the real world. The 21st century economy agrees with you. Once the dominant field in early AI research, it has since fallen somewhat out of favor compared to the much more practical subjects covered in the previous sections. Symbolic AI these days is not so much a standalone field as it is an academic approach for other forward-looking applications of narrow AI.

Of course, profitability is not always equivalent to importance. For all of the recent success in application-specific narrow AI, it is clear that *something* is missing in the quest to achieve true intelligence. I was jokingly critical of the brilliant early AI researchers from my privileged position as a mediocre citizen of the 21st century. But they weren't necessarily wrong.

·   ·   ·

Although movement and vision are part of the package, they are not what make human intelligence unique. What sets us apart from other lifeforms is our ability to invent and reason with profoundly abstract concepts. What makes us special is the fact that that men like Euclid, Newton, and Turing could inscribe on paper that which would someday become the pillars that bear civilization.

No combination of data-driven statistical methods have means to recreate this side of human intelligence, at least not yet. There's probably a chance that true reasoning ability might accidentally fall into existence when the various fields of narrow AI become much more mature and integrated. For now, symbolic AI seems to be our best hope.

Perhaps someday, the original dream of the 1950s will be fulfilled and the right combination of formal mathematical symbols, materialized in code and silicon, will be enough to trigger the spark of artificial consciousness. There probably won't be much warning given the theoretical nature of the work. But if that day comes, you can bet everything you own that the winds of change won't be so much a steady current as it will be a hurricane.

Prelude to Machine Learning

The past couple of chapters has covered some of the most important technical subjects in AI. Using this knowledge, you will have almost all of the technical foundation you'll need to appreciate the rest of this book as well as current mainstream AI news. However, I made one glaring omission up to this point: machine learning. Why? Because it deserves its own chapter.

Machine learning is far and away the hottest buzzword in the highly buzzword-y world of AI. It's the newest wave of technology that's revolutionizing just about every subfield. In the computer vision section, I only listed steps for the more traditional approach. In the NLP section, I was pretty vague about the technical process altogether. The truth is that both of these fields, like many other subcategories of AI, have been fully swept up in the machine learning craze. Robotics might not be far away.

Machine learning is about one thing and one thing only: data. We have no shortage of that here in the 21st century. As a result, whereas older AI research relied on clever hand-crafted algorithms, modern approaches try to extract solutions naturally from data itself. This has proven to be a massive paradigm shift. So, what exactly is machine learning? What kind of black magic does it use? Tune in next chapter to find out!

Reflections

1. What kinds of speech patterns do you regularly hear that might be problematic for computers to process?
2. In the robotics problem, the final step looks a little similar to the traveling salesman problem.

Does this task seem easier, harder, or equally as hard to you?

3. Do you believe that general intelligence and consciousness can be described by logic and math? (hint: this is a completely rhetorical question)

MACHINE LEARNING

*"Any sufficiently advanced technology is indistinguishable
from magic."*
- Arthur C. Clarke

Machine learning is, to date, the defining technology of 21st century AI. To many people, the name itself has some unsettling connotations. What's more human than the ability to learn? If a set of programs are going to spin wildly out of control and take over the world, then surely they would have ominous names like "deep neural networks" or "genetic algorithms". The important thing to remember is that many of these terms are mostly metaphors that happen to be pure gold for marketing purposes.

In reality, machine learning can be best described as a collection of advanced statistical methods. The underlying purpose is to describe a set of old data points in a way that can be used to say something useful about future data points. We call this description the *model* and refer to the old data as the *training set*. The measurable values associated with each data are called *features*.

If you think this goal sounds a lot like plain old statistics, you would be right. The distinction between the two fields is far from clear. However, there are two key characteristics that describes much of what people refer to as machine learning:

1. The problem is especially "hard" by our AI definition of hard.
2. The solution is highly integrated. It combines multiple steps into one black-box solution that accepts raw inputs.

We'll be discussing various types of machine learning problems in this chapter and their significance. It may seem like magic at times, but the applications are quite real.

Supervised Learning

The most widespread use of machine learning at the moment is called supervised learning. In supervised learning, every data point has a large number of features and a single final output that we are interested in trying to predict. For a concrete example, let's consider an algorithm that tries to predict prices on real estate sales. The first thing we need is a massive database of historical real estate listings. In this database, each data point is a single house that's characterized by features such as the square footage, number of bedrooms, and whether or not it has a garage. The output we are interested in predicting is the final selling value.

Supervised learning owes its name to the fact that the output of the training data needs to be known ahead of time. We can only predict future housing sales if the historical data is labeled with the right selling price. Since a human needs to enter the final price of each home at some point or another, they can be thought of as "supervising" the learning process.

This particular real estate example is a very important real world problem. However, it still feels fairly straightforward, as if machine learning is just a more accurate way to solve problems that we can already intuitively solve. It doesn't take a genius to put together an basic equation stating that larger houses with garages should cost more than smaller houses with no garage.

The real power of supervised learning is more apparent when it is extended to problems which were borderline unsolvable before. Take the most basic problem from computer vision: image recognition. The task is to come up with a systematic strategy to separate pictures of cats from pictures of other animals. Can you think of any easy places to start? I sure can't. Pictures of cats aren't colored or contrasted much differently from other pictures. You can't compare pixels individually because no two cats will be posing in the exact same position with the exact same lighting.

And yet, when Google engineers shove thousands and thousands of human-labeled animal pictures through a supervised learning algorithm, *somehow* the algorithm manages to do an excellent job of separating cats from non-cats. It processes each pixel as a different feature, eventually recognizes eyes, whiskers, and paws along the way, and outputs a stunningly accurate result. In this particular case, the most popular technique is *deep learning*, which itself is based on a type of data structure called a *neural network.*

Researchers have tried to dig into these models to see if they can analyze the real world representations. This is no easy task. More often than not, it's also totally beside the point. From image detection to speech recognition and bioinformatics, the appeal of these algorithms often begin and end as black-boxes, fundamentally unknowable models with immensely useful results.

A Note on Data Labeling

In supervised learning problems, labeling training data is often the bottleneck for both time and money. Bright, young graduate students across the world have spent countless hours mindlessly sorting between pictures of cats and raccoons. It also happens to lead to some of the most fascinating non-technical consequences of AI in the real world.

. . .

Take captchas for an example. Over the past few years, one of the more common variants displays an image and asks the user to identify objects within the pictures. If you've come across these tests, have you ever wondered why the target objects are almost *always* things like street signs and cars? I'll give you a hint: it's no coincidence that the Google, the company behind these captcha tests, also happens to be the industry leader in machine learning for street maps and self-driving cars.

This is just one example of an unexpected economic consequence in the machine learning revolution. For a totally different example, take a look at Amazon's Mechanical Turk business, a crowdsourcing platform with hundreds of thousands of workers whose primary purpose seems to be labeling supervised learning data. As our daily lives become more and more integrated into the digital world, I have no doubt that tech companies will find increasingly clever ways to make the most of their human livestock.

Unsupervised Machine Learning

In contrast with supervised learning, unsupervised learning addresses a different problem altogether. Algorithms in this subfield are designed to work with a set of data points that don't have any final output values at all, only features. As the name implies, there is no need for expensive human-labeled inputs.

The unsupervised learning problem is the following: given a collection of unlabeled data points, what is the best way to categorize them into logically related groups? One of the more straightforward applications deals with the design of search engines. Suppose that a search engine has a database of the following news articles covering reality TV stars Alice and Bob:

- Alice joins Bob on New Mexican tour
- Bob and Alice head to New Mexico
- Alice buys a new purse, it's blue!
- What does Alice's blue purse mean for her marriage?
- Alice and Bob say "hola amigos!" to New Mexican everywhere

Now, when avid fans search for news on Alice, they don't want a thousand articles about her vacation or a thousand articles about her purse. They want a little bit of everything going on in her life. As a result, the search engine needs some automatic way to categorize the articles in to separate, logically related groups. This calls for a *clustering algorithm.* The clustering algorithm will read through each article and automatically decide which articles resemble which. It doesn't need to understand the concept of vacations or purses at all, just that articles from each category seem to be talk about the same thing.

Anomaly detection in cybersecurity is another excellent application of unsupervised learning. Here, an administrator is interested in detecting whether weird, potentially malicious activity is occurring within a large computer network. You can think of the unsupervised learning algorithm as trying to classify between normal and abnormal behavior, whatever that might mean.

Other uses of unsupervised learning include consumer profiling in marketing applications and assorted data analysis, perhaps for academic or business intelligence purposes. Although the range of everyday applications are not quite as diverse as with supervised learning, you can see that these techniques are important for a number of fairly influential industries.

Reinforcement Learning

While supervised and unsupervised learning have taken the AI landscape by storm, they appear to be nearing diminishing returns as far as technical innovation is concerned. Reinforcement learning, on the other hand, is just now in its infancy in the real world.

This set of algorithms deals with a more dynamic type of problem in which the program uses data to make a series of decisions. Some excellent examples are the various games we talked about in Chapter 2: chess and Go. The reinforcement terminology comes from the fact that the AI has the opportunity to learn from its mistakes only after it has made the decision. In other words, the original strategy is *reinforced* by an observable future outcome.

. . .

One of the more amazing displays of this approach was the the victory of Google's AlphaGo program. AlphaGo initially trained by using a database of real games played by humans in the past. But then it did something amazing. It learned how to beat the very humans that it was trying to mimic. How is that possible? How did the student become the master? The answer: reinforcement learning.

After digesting the initial seed database, AlphaGo played countless more games against itself, introducing new variations to the strategy with every passing game. Thanks to the well-defined goals of the problem, it could improve its playing ability by reinforcing successful tactics and moving toward increasingly better and more innovative strategies. These types of processes are sometimes described as *evolutionary algorithms* because they mirror behaviors of natural selection seen in nature . The end result was a formidable, perfectly-tuned AI player whose alien behavior proved to be too sophisticated for the best that humanity had to offer.

We are only beginning to scratch the surface for other practical decision-making applications in diverse areas like robotics and interactive education. If you're more interested in profitability, then you may want to take special note of the fact that reinforcement learning is perfectly suited for financial asset trading as well. By all accounts, this subfield has a bright future indeed.

Algorithms vs Data

We've now covered all three major types of machine learning. One last point worth discussing is the interplay between algorithms and data. In machine learning, we have some very impressively named algorithms. As the names imply, neural networks draw inspiration from neurons while evolutionary algorithms draw inspiration from the way that organisms evolve through natural selection. The resemblances are quite beautiful. However, any time an engineering solution claims to be inspired by nature, you can assume two things:

1. The problem is incredibly difficult.
2. There's not really a right answer.

These are just two of a large number of algorithms within the machine learning field, most of which have the misfortune of having boring names like *support vector machine* or *k-nearest neighbors*. None are objectively better than their alternatives in every situation. Almost all have been around since the 1980s.

And so, we reach the most important lesson of this chapter. The modern machine learning revolution isn't about the algorithms. It's about the data. Here in the 21st century, companies have access to gargantuan troves of personal data that the 1980s could have only dreamed about. This is part of the reason that personal data has become such an important public policy problem.

It's no longer possible for an aspiring machine learning startup to challenge Google, Facebook, or Amazon on a purely technical level. No matter which interchangeable algorithm is used, no matter the amount of incremental improvements or fine tuning, bigger data will win every single time. For better or worse, machine learning belongs to the giants of the tech industry now. And they've built quite a world with it.

Now that you're familiar with machine learning, you should have a better appreciation for the state-of-the-art in AI technologies. Congratulations! Celebrate, relax, order a drink with Siri. For the remainder of this book, we'll be using this technical foundation to explore the rest of the story. We begin with a tour of the modern AI landscape and a glimpse of the world that awaits.

Reflections

1. Compare the process for categorizing cat pictures from *Supervised Learning* with the more traditional steps from *Computer Vision* in Chapter 3. Which of these steps are replaced by machine learning?
2. When clustering news articles for a search

engine, would you expect that each group has about the same number of articles?

3. A requirement of reinforcement learning is that we have an obvious way to measure success. For financial asset trading, what would make a good measurement?

AI IN DAILY LIFE

"People worry that computers will get too smart and take over the world, but the real problem is that they're too stupid and they've already taken over the world."
   -Pedro Domingos

Most people understand that AI is an interesting engineering problem, but not everyone realizes how it affects their daily life at every turn. If this describes you, then either you subscribe to religious beliefs banning the use of technology, or you just haven't been paying attention. That's what this chapter is for. From Siri to drones and robo-tutors, we'll be doing a casual meet-and-greet of the many different AI that you can expect to encounter in your daily life today.

Personal Devices

Let's start with the portal to the digital world: phones, tablets, and computers. If you're logging onto a modern mobile device, you've most likely already triggered an AI algorithm. This is because biometrics like fingerprint scanners, face scanners, and retinal scanners all require computer vision to securely identify your body parts.

Next, you'll want to enter in some type of input to the device. No matter which type of input you choose, some flavor of AI will be involved. Typing invokes autocorrect and intelligent word suggestions with adaptive NLP. Speaking to your phone invokes speech recognition software. Taking pictures often involves rudimentary computer vision. AI cannot be escaped.

After all of that, you finally get to interact with the AI superstars of the world: Alexa, Cortana, Google AI, and Siri. Clearly, these personal assistants need some pretty sophisticated NLP to even understand your commands. However, that's not all. Think about the reason that these personal assistants exist in the first place. With every passing year, our digital lives are getting more and more complicated. Whereas email used to be the only thing that people cared about, people today need to manage multiple social media accounts, gigabytes of data, ecommerce, media subscriptions, and a growing collection of Internet of Things (IoT) devices.

Companies have invested heavily in personal assistants to take care of the more mundane tasks on your behalf. To handle this job, programs must develop an excellent database of symbolic AI which understands concepts like email, calendars, smart thermostats, etc. The end goal is perfect efficiency. With some luck, we might never need to use our stubby thumbs again.

The Internet

Personal devices in the 21st century are really just a way to access The Internet, where three types of business reign supreme: search engines, video streaming, and social media. In fact, as of this writing, the top three most visited websites in the world are Google, Youtube, and Facebook. AI is key to all three business models.

We'll start with video streaming. Although high-quality content is the most important factor for success, a close second is the ability to connect the right content with the right people. Enter *recommender systems*. As the name implies, these programs are responsible for suggesting new and interesting videos for users based on their past behavior. Recommender systems are prominently powered by machine learning algorithms and can be extended to many other business models including news, music, and ecommerce.

In social networking, AI pops up in all kinds of strange places. Sites like Facebook and Instagram are interested in computer vision for tagging users while Snapchat is more concerned with how to decorate your face with weird filters. Twitter and Reddit are crawling with *bots*, dumb AI programs that pretend to be real human users. Companies are also very interested in analyzing the social networks themselves. A statistical analysis of your social life reveals all sorts of useful information that can be used for targeted advertising and, more disturbingly, for influencing public opinion.

. . .

Facebook and Youtube are great, but for technology ideal-ists, The Internet is really about knowledge. We've already mentioned a few search engine applications, namely image recognition and clustering. However, this only scratches the surface. At the end of the day, search engines are all about conveying information in the most efficient way: a task diffi-cult even for humans. Here is a quote by Google co-founder Larry Page back in 2000:

"Artificial intelligence would be the ultimate version of Google. The ultimate search engine that would understand everything on the web. It would understand exactly what you wanted and it would give you the right thing. We're nowhere near doing that now. However, we can get incrementally closer to that, and that is basically what we're working on."

Healthcare

The perfect all-purpose search engine does not exist at the moment. However, certain specific industries have made impressive progress in automated knowledge dissemination. Watson, IBM's victorious Jeopardy playing program, has been adapted to tackle some of the most important chal-lenges in healthcare. Its goal is to act as an advanced search engine for doctors as they make life-changing diagnosis and treatment decisions.

Watson's first advantage is that it has access to more raw medical knowledge than any human doctor can hope to memorize. However, even more importantly, AI like Watson will be better equipped to treat people as unique individuals. It will have instant access to personal medical history and real-time input from monitoring devices. It will interact with programs like "Medical Sieve", another AI from IBM that uses computer vision to analyze x-ray images. Perhaps most impressively, it will someday be able to talk to one of the many AI startups working to intelligently parse DNA sequences.

What does all of this mean? In essence, the massive amounts of data generated by modern healthcare is too much for even the most capable humans to process. The role of AI is to consolidate all of this information in a way that will allow physicians to finally treat each human body as what it really is: a unique and complex system that is much, much more than the sum of its parts.

It's only a short leap from there before the technology is made available to the patients directly. In a not too distant future, AI will be able to provide affordable, comprehensive, and personalized medical care for the general public.

Education

Education is another deeply personal field that seems ripe for change. Let's start with one of the most tedious task for human teachers: grading. Recently, test pilots for essay grading AI have received a lot of attention for standardized testing environments. Early studies have found that these programs can almost perfectly replace human graders, which is arguably a more indicative statement about standardized testing than about AI.

Nevertheless, essay grading remains a controversial application. Less daring AI companies prefer to focus on objective subjects like math. Their programs use a combination of computer vision and simple symbolic AI to more efficiently grade handwritten assignments.

Although automated grading will do wonders for efficiency, the real holy grail in educational AI is automated tutoring. The ideal AI tutor is an interactive chatbot that can conversationally assist students in their studies. Today, dozens of startups have designed a variety of tutoring tools for subjects ranging from math to foreign languages. Just like with medical advice AI, tutoring chatbots will soon provide tireless 24/7 feedback for students everywhere.

Educational AI will be extremely useful in traditional school environments. However, I'm betting that they will have an even more meaningful impact on the open online courseware movement. In this realm, cheap tutors and automated translation will be instrumental in spreading first-world education to the less privileged parts of the world. The opportunities are there, and it's hard to think of a more worthwhile application.

Transportation

Transportation is probably one of the most underrated human needs. Our anatomy reflects a unique ability among the animal kingdom to run far and free. Our roads represent freedom, exploration, and the enduring human desire to transcend the circumstances of our birthright. And yet, not a single one of these thoughts usually comes to mind when the average person fires up a boring GPS app.

People aren't very appreciative of the massive amount of work that goes into good navigation and transportation. Google street cars and satellites roam around all day taking endless pictures that are stitched together with computer vision. Real-time traffic data is being aggregated and updated nonstop. Afterwards, some combination of symbolic AI, machine learning, and proprietary black magic is used to flawlessly identify the fastest route to your destination.

Navigation just works. In fact, it works so well that recent studies suggest it may cause a decrease in human brain size. But that's beside the point.

Afterall, who needs a full-sized brain when self-driving cars are just on the horizon? Perhaps no acute AI application has caused as much excitement in recent years. This is evident in the number of tech giants all vying for control of the emerging market. Each one is betting on their unique competitive advantage: Google with their navigation dominance, GM and Ford with their automobile expertise, and Tesla with their Elon Musk.

Of course, transportation is as much about moving goods as it is about moving people. As automobile companies begin manufacturing self-driving trucks for transporting large shipments from city to city, companies like Amazon will be more interested in developing vast networks of drones to make that final delivery right to your house.

Autonomous vehicles are a remarkable achievement of robotics and computer vision. They are unique among other modern AI applications in that they very strongly affect the physical word, creating endless economic potential and endless political headaches for policy makers everywhere. Once they've arrived, there will be no mistaking that the AI revolution is well underway.

Security

The final broad area that's been highly affected by AI is one that I'll group under the umbrella term of "security". Security is loosely defined here as the task of making sure that things don't go wrong. It often goes unnoticed and underappreciated, but it affects almost every aspect of our lives.

We'll start with computer security. As pre-gmail internet users know, spam detection has come a very long way in filtering out annoying and dangerous messages. If you get targeted by computer viruses, cybersecurity companies are now using machine learning neural nets to find and stop malware. Banks employ anomaly detection systems to predict financial fraud. All of our standard security technologies will soon be integrated by AI in the ongoing struggle to keep data and digital identities safe from cyber-criminals.

Security extends to dangers in the real world as well. Is Robocop coming anytime soon? Probably not. However, surveillance, both in the traditional video camera sense and the more modern digital monitoring sense, is benefiting a lot from computer vision and statistical machine learning.

Robo-paramedic is even closer to becoming a reality. Due in part to its vulnerable geographic location, Japan has emerged a leader in the field of search and rescue robots. These machines are especially fascinating given the diversity of shapes and sizes ranging from fish-like submarines to snake-like robots designed to crawl through damaged rubble.

Finally, there's no security like national security. Unsurprisingly, the U.S. government is a major player in research on military robotics and AI. I'm sure entire books can and have been written about these applications. We won't try to come up with a full list here, but some of the more interesting highlights known to the public are weapon tracking systems, NLP for foreign intelligence, combat drones, and those insanely cool quadrupedal robots from Boston Dynamics. Whatever your views may be on the weaponization of technology, many of the most important advances in AI have been fueled by military funding. It seems unlikely that this will change any time soon.

The Best of the Rest

AI is a highly diverse field with a seemingly infinite number of applications. Much of the challenge in learning AI is simply an exercise in finding logical ways to group them together. Although I've done my best to highlight the major industries in this chapter, there are many others that don't quite fit into nice categories.

For instance, IBM's Watson, on top of its duties in health-care and education, has also taken on the task of inventing and selling new recipes as a cook. NLP software can now produce generic news articles. Similar projects are developing AI to produce music for movie soundtracks. These days, AI isn't so much limited by its technical circuitry, but by the creativity of its human programmers. All of this harkens back to a reflective question from Chapter 1, namely: what *isn't* AI? The question may seem no more clear than it was then. If it's any consolation, I'm sure someone will train a neural network to answer the question soon enough.

However, even these applications only tell half of the story. The AI mentioned in this chapter are just the half that you get to interact with personally. Your everyday experiences can be deceiving. In the next Chapter, we'll next take at look at everything going on behind the scenes, at the invisible army of AI programs working to power business and to unleash the new global economy.

Reflections

1. Of the applications listed, which ones have goals that strike you to be especially difficult from an AI perspective? Why?
2. In which of these applications can you argue that AI is currently not the biggest bottleneck, i.e. there is some other factor other than software that restricts how well the AI can do its job?
3. All of these applications have something in common: namely that they have at least a remote chance of becoming profitable. Do you have any economically useless but interesting ideas that you would like to see developed?

APPLICATIONS OF AI TO BUSINESS

"AI will probably most likely lead to the end of the world, but in the meantime, there'll be great companies."
  - Sam Altman

I n 1991, the U.S. military launched a program called DART, The Dynamic Analysis and Replanning Tool. DART was focused on a classic problem in AI called scheduling, which deals with the task of planning complicated logistics and was a crucial part of U.S. operations throughout the Gulf Coast War. DART was, by all measures, a raging success. After just four years, the money saved by the program had made up for everything the U.S. military had put into AI research over the previous 30 years combined.

AI today is being developed more by private businesses than the government. However, the lesson is clear: it's all about the money. We'll now take a look into how AI is starting to shape the basic backbone of business across every industry.

This chapter won't be able to cover every facet, of course. So, to help provide some structure, I'll break things down into the follow roles, a sort of "business for dummies" model:

1. *Making things* - manufacturing and production
2. *Selling things* - advertising and sales
3. *Housekeeping* - accounting, customer service, administration, IT
4. *Finding new things to make* - business strategy
5. *Raising money to make new things* - investment, asset trading

At the end of the day, AI, and technology in general, is driven by money. In every stage of business, AI is working hard and fast to improve some jobs, destroy others, and make just about everything a hell of a lot more profitable.

Making Things

There are a number of ways that AI helps to improve production. For instance, company supply chains benefit from the very same logistics and scheduling techniques that helped the U.S. win the Gulf Coast War. Different industries have different ways of leveraging data science. Fossil fuel companies use it in geological surveying, agriculture uses it for crop monitoring, and renewable energy uses it for weather prediction.

These are all excellent use cases, but let's get straight to the point. If we're going to talk about "making things", then we should really talk about *making things*. In this regard, AI has one supremely useful offering, and that's robotics.

Robots have been a key component in the manufacturing industry long before AI became relevant. These were dumb machines that could only repeat a single pre-programmed motion over and over. The modern wave of "smart" robots, on the other hand, are equipped with sensors and multi-functional hardware capable of performing many different tasks. They can often navigate around complex buildings like an Amazon warehouse or use tools that were originally made for humans.

Modern "cobots" (collaborative robots), as they are called, are designed to interact safely and productively with their human counterparts. A great example of a commercially available cobot is the humanoid named Baxter. Baxter has elastic joints which yield to human contact and a cute digital face that can convey basic emotions for feedback. When Baxter needs to learn a new job on the assembly line, human coworkers can simply guide its arms in the correct motion to "teach" it the new task. Smart robots like Baxter are not yet the norm, but the use cases are growing rapidly.

Even industries which are typically less associated with cutting edge technology have warmed up to robots. In agriculture, robots have been recruited to pick fruit, administer pesticides, and even shear sheep. All of these tasks require a high degree of sophisticated computer vision and navigation to deal with the annoying lack of straight lines and right angles found in the outdoors. In the energy sector, ExxonMobil is actively collaborating with about 80 different universities across the world. The goal? To develop submarine robots for deep-sea exploration in search of oil.

One last noteworthy use of robotics occurs in healthcare production. In the pharmaceutical industry, the same motion planning algorithms described in Chapter 3 are surprisingly applicable to drug creation. Recall that motion planning AI deals with how different parts of a robot can be coordinated to move from point A to point B. In drug creation, the same exact algorithms can explore how different parts of a protein are moved around to attach to other molecules. This unexpected crossover is yet another illustration of AI as a powerful cross-industry tool.

Although robotics is just one of the many faces of AI, it will always be the most visible. As the various breeds of digital AI fade in and out of popular interest, smart industrial robots will remain and grow as an enduring symbol of the changing economy.

Selling Things

Making useful products is only part of the battle when it comes to day-to-day business operations. The process of advertising and selling products to end users may see an even larger benefit from AI in the near future. To provide some historical context, here is my favorite quote from the advertising world:

Half the money I spend on advertising is wasted; the trouble is I don't know which half.

This quote is attributed to marketing pioneer John Wanamaker, who died in 1922. Since then, things sure have changed. The customer data available in today's world is an informational paradise for marketers everywhere. Social media, search engines, and real-time browsing behavior are all woven together by advertising firms into vivid profiles of potential customers.

The rise of e-commerce means that purchases can be digitally monitored and factored back into the equation, closing the information loop. In other words, not only can businesses send out more effective targeted advertising, they can actually see which ads lead to sales and which do not. Somewhere in Philadelphia, John Wanamaker must be dancing in his grave.

AI lies at the core of this entire process. The high-level technical steps are simple enough. First take all of the information you have about a given user and shove it through a machine learning algorithm. This predicts the likelihood that the user will be receptive to a particular type of advertisement. Monitor the user to see whether they click on the advertisement or buy the product. Feed the result back into the algorithm to improve accuracy. Rinse and repeat.

. . .

AI also affects a second level of advertising. One of the many fascinating consequences of marketing in The Internet Age is that advertisers need to constantly bid for ad space in a process called RTB (real time bidding). This extremely frequent bidding process occurs on a per-user basis. It is done automatically and, surprise, surprise, with the help of machine learning. This time, the process involves a reinforcement learning approach.

When combined with the first customer profiling step, the result is a rather beautiful two-layer process that considers both a user's baseline potential as a customer as well as the cost of their attention at any given moment.

Advertising is only half the battle when it comes to selling products. The second half is, of course, actually selling things. AI has made many impacts on this front as well by making the experience easier for users. However, I would argue that the most important development is the potential for firms to implement price discrimination for different customers buying the same product. Although it is illegal now, a future that allows for widespread price discrimination would have enormous economic ramifications for consumers and the growing rate of wealth inequality.

Housekeeping

The final component of day-to-day operations is what I'll informally refer to as the housekeeping component. This includes all support groups that are needed to keep a business running smoothly. The impact of AI in these areas is not as neatly summarized as in production or sales. Instead, you can think about it as a collection of different tools to make each task more efficient. We'll do a quick run through of some important examples.

Accounting & Legal - NLP algorithms will reduce a lot of the initial manpower involved in crunching through large amounts of documents. In accounting, this means auditing. In legal, this means searching for relevant laws and court cases. Reduced manpower, of course, means extra savings for companies.

Customer Service - Chatbots and automated call centers are the key technologies here. These intelligent programs can cut costs by more efficiently redirecting problems to the right humans and even solving the more easy problems themselves.

Human Resources - One of the most time consuming tasks in human resources occurs during recruitment. AI can help companies reduce the work by screening employees ahead of time with NLP and machine learning. Unfortunately, this raises some tricky questions concerning various types of discrimination.

Information Technology - These days, there's no hotter topic in IT than cybersecurity and there's no hotter buzzword in cybersecurity than AI. As IT networks get larger, it's becoming difficult for human experts to monitor every corner of the system. Machine learning can help with dynamic tasks like anomaly detection as well as more static tasks like auditing IT components for safety before they are deployed.

Whereas AI in advertising and sales seem to enable brand new opportunities for business, housekeeping AI are often framed by how they can save time and money for companies. Often, these savings come in the form of lost jobs. Again, this has potential for both positive and negative economic consequences which we'll explore in Chapter 8.

Finding New Things to Make

We now arrive at the top of the business food chain, to the men and women calling the shots at the highest levels of business. For all of their expensive suits and inflated salaries, CEOs and other high-ranking executives are no more immune to the winds of change than the rest of us.

Strategic business decisions are more data-driven than ever before. Emerging market exploration, price determination, product differentiation, acquisitions, and lobbying decisions are all built on intensive data analytics. The tools involved are the usual suspects: NLP for crunching reports and machine learning for predicting potential outcomes. I won't belabor the technical details at this point. What's far more interesting to consider is how AI will change the makeup of business leaders heading into the future.

. . .

On the one hand, a baseline level of technical competence is clearly needed. High-ranking executives don't always have the best track record for embracing technological change. There's a reason that tech startups love to drone on about "disrupting" rather than "incrementally out-competing" the status quo. However, if capitalism still works, then we would expect that companies which embrace sound AI strategies will eventually do better in the long run.

On the other hand, some experts think that the current trend toward "softer" skills for executive roles will only increase. As AI becomes better at performing hard cognitive tasks, human traits like leadership and emotional intelligence will become more valuable than traditional IQ.

For now, the Jeff Bezoses of the world are still earning their money. AI is simply a strategic tool that can be used to aid humans decision makers. But as these tools become increasingly sophisticated, who knows what the job of an executive will look like in the future? Jack Ma, co-founder and chairman of Alibaba predicts that a robot CEO will outperform his human colleagues in 30 years. The good 'ol boys club might be well on its way to becoming the good 'ol bots club.

Raising Money to Make New Things

You can't talk about the modern economy without a mention of Wall Street and stock trading. Most companies don't need to worry about it directly, but at the end of the day, a company's ability to grow is directly related to how Wall Street values its shares. More so than just about any other application we've discussed, AI and trading is a match made in heaven. Let me explain why. Here are three key properties that you can use to characterize most AI problems:

1. *Purity* - the inputs and goals are well-defined within the digital world
2. *Value* - the solution has a real economic impact
3. *Competition* - there's a constant need to outperform some opponent or adversary

The majority of AI problems that we've covered only have one or two of these properties. For instance, chess playing AI have purity and competition but next to no economic *value*. Cybersecurity applications have obvious value and are in constant competition to outsmart hackers, but the random behavior of human employees ruins the digital *purity* of the problem. Finally, image recognition software has pretty good purity and value, but there's no intense *competition*. An algorithm that can identify images with 99.9% accuracy is only marginally better than one with a 99.8% accuracy.

In contrast, financial trading is one of those rare AI problems that beautifully combines all three properties. The economic value is obvious, the trading interactions are well defined, and relentless competition between hedge funds is leading toward an all-out race to the top. I expect that this killer combination will drive stock trading AI to very quickly outpace many other applications going forward. So how does it work?

Even if you're not familiar with stock trading, you've probably heard of the mantra "buy low and sell high". Easier said than done. For centuries, the most successful traders had passed down special strategies to predict future stock value by looking for patterns and correlations in the price data. They relied on the fact that a majority of the less skilled participants in the markets acted in psychologically predictable ways by panicking in certain scenarios and getting greedy in others. This strategy is called "technical analysis" and was highly effective through the 20th century.

Today, AI has totally destroyed traditional technical analysts in the stock market. Computers can remember infinitely more historical data, learn more sophisticated patterns, and make perfectly rational decisions all within a fraction of a second. We humans evolved to spot ravenous man-eating tigers, not lines on a financial graph.

Advanced technical analysis is a very straightforward application of stock trading AI. Of course, it doesn't mean that all human traders have gone out of business; there's a lot more that goes into evaluating stocks than just pattern recognition. Analysts need to aggregate all kinds of loosely related information including company finances, general market conditions, and the progress of global technology, to name a few. AI clearly isn't at a point where it can completely replace this kind of human intelligence.

However, as information about companies and economies are becoming more accessible in the digital world, the advantage of natural human intelligence is slowly losing ground to cold, calculated pattern recognition. It won't be long before AI start to consult current events in Greece before buying shares of a Chinese firm from an American hedge fund. The players are ready, the pieces are in place, and the race to dominate Wall Street is on.

———

Between chapters 5 and 6, we've now covered just about every major aspect of AI in the modern world. You've probably noticed by now that AI affects a lot of different industries. The best I could do in this book was to make general statements that provide a rough idea of the scope and higher-level trends. If any of the more specific areas have peaked your curiosity, then perhaps you would be interested in doing your own research. Endless information is only a quick AI-supported Google search away.

So, rather than churning up more examples, we're going to move on to the next broad section of the book: looking into the future. What types of technology are already heading down the academic research pipeline? How might we begin to understand the potential significance? Keeping up with

AI calls for staying a step ahead of the curve, and that's exactly what we'll be doing next.

Reflections

1. In the customer profiling step of advertising AI, what kind of machine learning do you think is being used (supervised, unsupervised, reinforcement)?

2. If someday entire companies can be run by AI CEOs, do you think there will be any jobs left for the people below them? Why or why not?

3. Suppose that a company has two types of robotic arms. One is a "dumb" robot that can only do pre-programmed motions. The second is a "smart" robot equipped with a camera as well as with state-of-the art computer vision and motion planning AI. What is one example of a production task that you might be able to do with second but not the first?

FUTURE TRENDS IN AI

"A lot of what AI is being used for today only scratches the surface of what can be done. It will become so ubiquitous that we won't even call it AI anymore." - Babak Hodjat

You've already seen how basic AI tools are beginning to change the world. At last, we get to what all of this is really about: the future. AI isn't so much a "what have you done for me lately" field as a "what are you going to do for me next" field. Whether you are a long-term opportunist, a starry-eyed student, or a prospective Silicon Valley fortune teller, this is the chapter for you.

Humans are notoriously bad at predicting the future. The history of AI presented in Chapter 1 was a fine example. As a result, it goes without saying that none of the specific applications in this chapter are ever guaranteed to see the light of day. Rather than leaving you with a collection of hit-or-miss predictions, I'll instead try to paint them into a single meaningful picture. Overall, the underlying prediction is this:

The next generation of AI will be about interactions.

AI as the science of beefed-up data analysis is already reaching diminishing returns on innovation. Moving forward, we will begin to measure the sophistication of AI programs by their ability to interact well with other intelligent parties. Here are the categories I would like to talk about:

- *AI → Human*
- *Human → AI*
- AI → AI
- AI → Adversary
- AI → Self

As I hope you'll see, this prediction about the future of AI won't turn out to be very bold at all. The most widely held theories of natural intelligence, such as the social brain hypothesis and social exchange theory, suggest that interactions are they key to understanding how our animal brains evolved. Accelerated by the blinding speed of digital communication, AI may soon benefit from the same quantum leap in true intelligence.

AI → Human

To many people, the very term of Artificial Intelligence implies a kind of attempt to replace humans and, by extension, human interaction. We've already seen a few good examples in Chapter 5 such as personal digital assistants and medical advice AI. While impressive in their own right, the programs that exist today don't provide much more than a slick way to interact with the same dumb computers. The future of AI → Human interaction is about creating rich, meaningful experiences that simply feel like real human contact.

There are a few challenges involved, the first of which has to do with long-term interactions. Modern AI is very good at answering single questions and performing single tasks. It's not quite as good at maintaining extended conversations. Another challenge deals with the ability to handle increasingly abstract topics. Modern AI is great at parroting straightforward facts, okay at making basic comparisons, and useless at understanding broad categories and high-level concepts. These types of abilities require a certain level of symbolic understanding of context and semantics that we haven't quite mastered at a large scale.

Better AI → Human interactions will lead to AI that seem more and more human. At first, it will greatly improve existing AI applications such as automated customer service and digital smartphone assistants. In the long run, it will enable brand new applications like home medical robots and, yes, sexually provocative chatbots.

. . .

However, the biggest changes will occur at a psychological level. Once we make enough progress, AI → Human interactions will fundamentally change the way we think about knowledge. It will make Google seem less like an idiot savant and more like a wise village elder that can answer the questions you didn't know you wanted to ask. Imagine that instead of holding a mere encyclopedia in the palm of your hand, you can hold your doctor, lawyer, teacher, and best friend all rolled into one. That will change everything indeed.

Human → AI

Whereas the previous section was about how AI will interact with humans in the human world, this section talks about humans entering the world of machines. Currently, we call these people "programmers".

One of the hottest areas of current research is called *program synthesis*. The idea is that human programmers will be able to make simple high-level specifications that will be automatically converted into computer code. While the field has been around for a while, it has seen a massive rise in popularity with new AI techniques that can learn programming patterns from the billions of lines of freely available code on The Internet. Perhaps coding software in languages like Java and C++ will someday seem as pointless as manually writing out 1's and 0's. Although program synthesis doesn't cut humans out of the loop entirely, the idea of "computer programs writing computer programs" never fails to spark attention-grabbing headlines.

At the opposite end of the spectrum, AI is making computers more accessible to non-coders as well. One effort from Carnegie Mellon called *conversational machine learning* is about allowing everyday users to program new features into AI using natural language. Normally, computer software can only be modified by opening up the source code to write changes. With conversational machine learning, users will be able to teach the program how to do new tasks just by talking to it. You won't have to wait for the next update to get that feature you've always wanted.

In both of these research areas, the rather ambitious goal is to replace traditional coders altogether. Imagine a future in which graphic designers can coax an AI into building beautiful websites without the help of human web developers. Imagine that CEOs can just scream at an Excel spreadsheet until it displays the right trendlines.

Notice that unlike in the previous section, none of these AI programs are trying to pass for humans. Instead, the idea is to make it easier for humans to interact with machines. The ultimate goal is to democratize technology, allowing normal people to regain a small measure of control in an increasingly machine-dominated world.

Ai → Ai

Alright, enough with annoying human interactions. It's a bit of a shame that so much research effort in AI is devoted to accommodating our horribly strange human behavior. Fortunately, there is an abundance of ongoing research in the clean, mathematical world of AI → AI interaction.

This is the study of *multi-agent* systems. The word "agent" in this case is just a technical term for an intelligent "thing" that has its own goals, strategy, and internal state. You and I are each individual agents. In a group of robots, each robot would be a separate agent. As the name implies, these are systems in which there are many different AI agents that interact in complex and often unpredictable ways.

These systems can be purely digital. In multi-agent mining, many copies of an AI program cooperate to explore different parts of the same dataset. These systems can also be physical, as is the case of swarm robotics. Swarm robotics itself is a fascinating field with applications ranging from military drone formations to more futuristic armies of medical nanobots that will someday navigate the human body looking for tumors and pathogens.

The common thread between all of these applications is coordination, cooperation, and communication between the various agents. The large number of dynamic relationships tend to result in stunning levels of complexity and weird

reach the even more terrifying militaristic arena of so-called "cyber warfare".

As mentioned in regards to the trading AI of Chapter 6, the importance of adversarial settings should not be underestimated. Competition is the breeding ground of innovation. In the natural world, it has led to the evolution of our best and worst behaviors. No doubt it will do the same for the next generation of AI.

AI → Self

The final set of interactions we're going to talk about will take place within a single AI agent. As we discussed in Chapter 3, you can loosely view each area of modern AI as working on its own narrowly focused aspect of intelligence. Computer vision, robotics, NLP, etc. are all trying to replicate one particular part of our human cognition. The next big step is to connect all of these functions in an intelligent way.

We already see some of this today in highly integrated systems like self-driving cars. However, most of the interaction seems to be fairly straightforward and easily described. In our own brains, it's clear that something much more interesting is going on.

Why is it that when you see a picture of your hometown, it triggers sounds and smells from your childhood memories? Why do other attractive human beings have the ability to cripple your otherwise logical thought process and make your nervous system go haywire? It's as if there's some higher level of coordination that is directing our lower cognitive abilities like a conductor directs a symphony.

Neither of these examples are particularly relevant for AI, but they evolved for very good reasons in our own species. One possible explanation is that brain power isn't infinite. It probably helps to be able to coordinate memories, sensory information, and actions in useful and strategic ways depending on the task at hand. Computing power isn't infinite either. As the AI systems of tomorrow become increasingly complex and integrated, they will benefit from the same type of sophistication.

Coordination between cognitive functions is only one of the many challenges that can be classified under the AI → Self umbrella. As the technology develops, perhaps AI will self-interact by modifying its own code to unlock adaptation and creativity. Advanced AI will require deep introspection and who knows, maybe even consciousness. These are all out of the scope of this current chapter, but it's clear that the AI → Self relationship will be a key ingredient to true intelligence. With computers as with humans, enlightenment must come from within.

From Technology to Impact

Once we shift toward the next generation of highly interactive AI, it might not be long before advances in one area suddenly prove to be useful for applications we never even knew we wanted. Maybe advanced tutoring chatbots can be tweaked to improve social skills in shy children. Perhaps methods developed by artificial life researchers will unexpectedly be relevant to new foreign policy theory. All of this is a direct result of the explosion in complexity that arises when previously isolated intelligent systems are combined in new and powerful ways.

If we can be sure of one thing, it's that AI will have far reaching consequences that extend beyond just the technological realm. In the next Chapter, we'll be talking all about the economic and political questions that have already begun to arise. Out here in the non-technical world, where most people live, things are about to become very different.

Reflections

1. One of these categories that we talked about (Human → AI, AI → Human, AI → AI, AI → Adversary, AI → Self) is very closely related to the Turing test. Which one is it?
2. If you could program your favorite AI assistant to learn new tasks by just talking to it, what are some operations that you would find useful? Hint: Keep in mind that main benefit of conversational machine learning is to empower you to build personal features that other users might not necessarily want.
3. If attackers could easily fool machine learning algorithms, what is an example of a problem they can cause in the near future?

THE POLITICS AND ECONOMICS OF AI

"I'm increasingly inclined to think that there should be some regulatory oversight, maybe at the national and international level, just to make sure that we don't do something very foolish. With artificial intelligence we're summoning the demon. You know those stories where there's the guy with the pentagram, and the holy water, and he's sure he can control the demon?

Doesn't work out."

\- Elon Musk, Tech Mogul

Have you ever noticed that most Sci-Fi movies about AI follow the same predictable character arc? In the first half of the movie, the very obviously smart, humanlike, and sentient AI spends most of its day getting berated by the insensitive human population. "You can't really feel anything," they say. "You're just a bunch of dumb code!". Then something changes. After a pivotal moment in the plot, one of the main characters has an sudden epiphany. Blessed with wisdom far ahead of the time, he/she finally realizes "Oh my God, you really *are* just like us!"

Somehow, a genre renown for its creativity can't be bothered to spend two seconds on a more convincing public opinion. People don't just stand around while technology develops. They talk about it. A lot. Here in the early 21st century, AI is barely out of the crib and we *already* can't stop hearing about how it's going to screw up modern society.

The best and worst is yet to come. I'll try to cover some of the more interesting and disturbing issues in this chapter. None have clear answers, but that is precisely what makes them so important. More so than any of the technological topics we've discussed, these are issues that you yourself will help shape as a member of society. And if someday you ever find yourself in a hollywood-esque encounter with a misunderstood AI, then hey, at least you saw it coming.

Life and Death

You're driving through an intersection with your brand new self-driving Tesla. Suddenly, a small group of adorable toddlers unwittingly wanders onto the road. The only way for the AI to avoid them is to swerve into the median, likely killing yourself and everyone in the car. What should it do?

Humans are used to the idea of technology having an accidental impact on life or death situations. Buildings collapse, cars malfunction, medicines create side effects. With AI, technology now has a newfound ability to make *active* decisions about the worth of a human life. This presents challenging policy questions. In the scenario above, should governments mandate that self-driving cars save as many lives as possible? Should some lives be more valued than others? Whatever the default policies are, skilled car hobbyists will probably be able to override it. Is that within their rights as a property owner or is it pre-planned manslaughter?

Related questions about life and death are growing in areas like healthcare and autonomous warfare as well. When machines gain the ability to do arithmetic on human life, the trail of responsibility becomes a lot more complicated. Inevitably, we are led back to the old libertarian adage: AI doesn't kill people, algorithmically implemented legal policy kills people.

Algorithmic Prejudice

When it's not directly causing death, AI is still affecting our lives at very critical stages. We've already talked about how machine learning is used to process job resumes. As another example, police are using AI to predict crime in dangerous areas. These are already ripe situations for racial and gender-based human prejudice. AI might just make things even worse.

There are many different sides to this rather delicate issue. On the one hand, AI is only as good as its data, which can reflect some pretty awful human behaviors. A famous incident occurred in 2016 when Microsoft configured a chatbot named Tay to learn from public input on twitter. Twitter being twitter, it took less than a day before Tay had to be shut down due to her newfound love for racism, questionable political ideas, and Hitler.

Despite the prevalence, bad human input is just the tip of the iceberg in this area. The far harder question is how to handle bias when bias is profitable. To a human, varying gender representation in the job market or racial correlations in crime rates might point to problems with society. To an AI, this is all extremely useful information.

That's a problem. Useful information leads to useful predictions, and useful predictions lead to more profits. Even if society collectively decides to fight algorithmic prejudice, it's unclear how we will be able to convince competitive businesses to purposely cripple their own products when it's the right thing to do. Dealing with twelve year old Facists on twitter is pretty easy in comparison.

Economic Challenges

Although social issues presented by AI are quite fascinating, nobody seems to know how important any single topic will be. Economics is a bit more of a complete story.

First, it's perfectly safe to say that AI will make just about everything cheaper. This is true of any new technology; if it doesn't improve business, then nobody would bother making it. The real question is how big the change will be. Is the modern generation of AI another dotcom bubble or is it the next industrial revolution? No doubt you wouldn't be reading this book if you didn't think there was a strong chance of the latter.

If AI delivers on everything that it promises, then the economic benefits are straightforward. As a result, we'll spend some time talking about the other, darker side of the story. This is a story of inequality. At every level of the economy, AI threatens to tear apart any semblance of wealth equality that we are still holding onto today. How we deal with this threat is perhaps the most important social challenge of our time.

Labor

The threat to the job market is the most talked-about consequence of AI. As the prediction goes, the rate of automation will outstrip our limited abilities to create new jobs. Soon most humans will be unemployed, leading to existential questions about how we can maintain equality and basic humans rights in an era where not everybody can make a living.

Although this is the most pressing problem, there's a second more subtle challenge. A recent study by the OECD and referenced by the Economist magazine lists the following jobs with the highest risk of being replaced by automation:

- Food preparation
- Construction
- Cleaning
- Driving
- Agricultural Labor
- Garment Manufacturing
- Personal Service
- Sales
- Customer Service
- Business Administration
- Information Technology

Oddly, some of these jobs are historically seen to be decent, high-paying professions. This is a very interesting trend. AI isn't necessarily going after the low-paying, undesirable jobs as commonly believed, but for jobs in the middle of the curve. Why is that?

For dramatic effect, I'll try to get the point across in the following made-up newspaper blurb:

Get ready folks! At the much anticipated Google I/O 2042 conference, Boston Dynamics finally unveiled the new CHL 2.0, the next in its line of advanced robots tailor-made for the modern work environment. This time, CHL 2.0 comes equipped with Turing-grade NLP software, an integrated vision system, and two, yes two, multi-functional manipulators that can handle almost any tool. Amazingly, they have decided to give away CHL 2.0 for FREE! For only a low bimonthly fee for fuel and maintenance, how can CHL 2.0 revolutionize YOUR business?

Sounds pretty groundbreaking, right? Yes, except that CHL really just describes a typical unskilled human person (Cheap Human Labor 2.0). With all of the recent advances, it's easy to forget that AI still pales in comparison to the real thing. And the real thing, in a lot of cases, can be had for minimum wage. Why bother with expensive machinery when state-of-the-art human beings are mass produced everyday? Accountants and managers may soon be replaced, but the busboys of the world aren't going anywhere.

The fact that AI will probably cause massive unemployment is bad enough. But if it manages to separate the human workforce into two distinct social classes along the way, then we have yet another problem on our hands, one with disturbingly dystopian undertones.

Capital

The other half of the AI inequality story is ownership. Since the wealthy own a disproportionately large share of corporations, they stand to benefit the most from both the increased profits and decreased labor costs.

This is of course a normal feature of capitalistic society. However, AI creates some new complications. In the near term, successful AI technology is capable of generating enormous profits for the same reason that all software can:

its growth is not limited by any finite physical resources. As was mentioned in Chapter 3, the machine learning industry in particular will always favor large companies that have access to the most user data.

The long term is much more concerning. If AI is a second industrial revolution, then the finish line is the point when all jobs are automated. AI programs themselves will design increasingly sophisticated manufacturing technologies to send the world economy into unimaginable levels of wealth and prosperity.

The first companies to reach the finish line hold the potential to absolutely dominate global GDP very quickly. At the center of attention will be the stockholders claiming legal ownership of these technologies.

What happens to them will be determined by society. Will we honor property rights, allowing the lucky stockholders to become financial gods of the new world? Will populist revolution take over just in time to turn AI into a public good? Or will the AI themselves earn some strange form of legal independence, freeing their production from the notion of ownership entirely? While these possibilities may seem outlandish, the seeds of change are already here and the questions are too important to ignore.

An Economic Solution

The moral of the story is that our current economic system is being attacked from every direction. To combat the growing threat of inequality many people are supporting a new brand of technological socialism. According to this mindset, mass unemployment is an inevitability, but the explosion in overall wealth means that nobody needs to starve a result.

Their proposed solution is to implement a Universal Basic Income (UBI). UBI is just a sum of money that's distributed freely to everyone to cover their basic living needs. It's the socialist dream at its finest. It's a pretty provocative suggestion, and public response to this idea seems to be divided into three camps:

Opponents - These economic purists tend to not see a problem at all. They maintain that historically, job market doomsday headlines have been around since the invention of the mechanical loom. The economy has adopted every single time and this time is no different.

Supporters - Supporters clearly believe that there is a problem, and that UBI is the best way to uphold our standards for human rights. On top of that, it would greatly simplify social welfare and provide a nice safety net for risky entrepreneurial pursuits.

. . .

Other - Finally, there are those who say that a problem exists, but UBI alone is not the answer. To members of this camp, a job represents more than just a paycheck, and UBI is no substitute for our deeply human need to find meaning in our daily lives.

I'll leave it up to you to decide which position you take, but for pure speculative purposes, I find concerns from the third camp to be the most interesting. Suppose that humanity really does move into a future without labor. What *will* people do with their time?

Recent studies into certain unemployment demographics suggest that video games and targeted entertainment could play a key role in maintaining life satisfaction. Weirdly specialized art driven through social media will likely explode. The end of labor also means the rise of perennially available eyeballs to stimulate. If AI is the most lucrative technology of the future, then a solid infrastructure for the new generation of human couch potatoes has got to be a close second.

Unknown Unknowns

I hope you're convinced by now that AI is about more than just the technology. We're in for a world of change, and the issues we've covered here still only represent the tip of the iceberg. The infinitely harder challenge is in dealing with issues that we don't know exist yet, the unknown unknowns, as people like to call them. Many of them will be similar in magnitude to the topics we've discussed here. One is not.

. . .

As history plays itself out, humanity marches ever closer to the greatest unknown unknown. There, beyond the limits of our wildest imagination lies something more pivotal than the birth of organic life and more alien than the most distant reaches of space: *Strong AI*

In the next and final chapter, we will discuss events leading up to this closing act in the story. Dreams of utopia and threats of apocalyptic disaster all end here. Strong AI is the most important technology humanity will ever develop, and one way or another, it will be our last.

Reflections

1. Banning race and gender input would probably not be enough to eliminate more traditional bias in most cases. What other pieces of typically correlated information can a machine learning algorithm use to infer race and gender indirectly?
2. Do you think that AI should ever be a public good or should it always belong to the organization that developed it?
3. How would you expect that you and your particular social group would spend your time if you never had to work again?

STRONG AI AND THE SINGULARITY

"I visualize a time when we will be to robots what dogs are to humans. And I am rooting for the machines." - Claude Shannon

Here it is: the final chapter. Up until now, the goal of this book has been to approach AI from a more practical perspective. Not anymore. These last few pages are all about how we will achieve strong, general AI and what happens next. At last, we are free to indulge in the real essence of AI: wild speculation, Sci-Fi fueled fantasies, and the fate of humanity.

Make no mistake: this isn't about saving the most fun chapter for last. It's about saving the most important. The reasons for this aren't strictly political, economical, or even technological. Although the future promises some incredible technological progress in fields like genetic engineering and nanotechnology, comparing these to AI is a bit like comparing your favorite hobbies to the task of raising your firstborn child. It's just not the same, and here are a few reasons why:

- Strong AI will eliminate our need to work, invent, and create
- Strong AI will force us to face deep questions about consciousness and souls
- Strong AI will carry out the human will to its logical extreme

No other man-made invention is in the same league as AI. One day, history will be divided into two parts: the time before and the time after the arrival of strong AI. All that remains to be seen is whether future society will even care about our half.

Paths to Strong AI

You could probably imagine an infinite number of ways that strong AI will eventually come to life. We'll classify the possibilities into three broad categories. As a lame coincidence, these can be remember these as the three (E)xits on the journey of AI.

Engineered - This is the first image that comes to mind when most people think about AI research. For all intents and purposes, you can imagine it like in the movies: a mad scientist toils away in his private lab and suddenly, he discovers the secret algorithm. By encoding knowledge and enabling the program to learn in just the right way, he unleashes the power of strong AI. The key takeaway is that it's an instantaneous event that can happen any time, anywhere.

Emergent - Here, strong AI isn't a deliberate creation that any single human can understand, but an emergent phenomenon that somehow spontaneously arises from the complex digital world. Maybe it's the result of endless trials of a genetic algorithm. Or maybe the Internet of the future will have so much computational power that some combination of randomness will magically trigger an emergent intelligence. It's unclear whether the event would be gradual or abrupt, but it seems highly likely that we won't even know when it happens.

Emulation - Finally, in the least elegant path imaginable, we could just scan the human brain in its entirety, emulating a virtual human intelligence. Advancing AI along this path would mean making educated tweaks of the emulated brain to gradually build improvements on nature's existing product. Of course, there might be some ethical concerns about carrying out fatal experiments on simulated humans... let's not worry about that for now.

It's probably the case that we'll see an exciting race between systems from all three approaches. However, some of these might be doomed from the start.

Engineered AI is probably the most uncertain approach.

Although we tend to assume that our understanding of neuroscience and AI will get better and better, perhaps there's some philosophical limit that prevents human intelligence from being able to understand and reinvent human intelligence, like trying to fit a box inside of itself. If that were case, our AI would eventually have an intelligence that was comparable to dogs or cats, but they would always lack that last jump toward what we consider to be "true" intelligence.

On the other hand, the possibility of whole-brain emulation is a good enough reason to believe that strong AI *will* come sooner or later. While the other two approaches depend on some serious breakthroughs in basic theory, emulation is more about good old fashioned incremental progress. Today, neuroscientists can already map all of the neurons in the brain of a fruit fly. This technology will only get better moving forward.

The result is that humans might not even need to understand how natural intelligence works in order to reproduce it. My name isn't Leonardo Da Vinci, but I can make a damn good photocopy of the Mona Lisa.

The Singularity

The arrival of human-level AI is very likely from a purely technical perspective. Already, the implications would be pretty staggering: mass unemployment, the need for AI civil rights, and an all around threat to humanity's rule of the world. Yet somehow, in this line of wild speculation and apocalyptic ravings, this is just the start. The more important part of the story goes like this:

Strong AI will be able to do many of the things that humans do, from law and medicine to teaching. One of these is engineering. Equipped with the robotic equivalent of a bachelor's degree in computer science, the first generation of AI 1.0 toils away to make modest improvements on its own design.

This goes well enough that AI 2.0 turns out to be slightly better at law, medicine, teaching, and of course, engineering! The fresh teams of AI 2.0 quickly proceed to make an even better AI 3.0. And so on. This process continues indefinitely until each new generation of AI is so smart that their thinking begins to outpace their human creators. We won't be able to keep up.

One instant, AI will be like an endless army of Albert Einsteins, each equipped with photographic memories and instant access to the web. A few generations later, their most basic thoughts will be incomprehensible to even the smartest of us. Finally, at what we will call "the end", the machines will be indistinguishable from gods. We will be to robots what dogs are to humans. The Earth will be home to its first superintelligence.

The superintelligence explosion can be triggered anywhere in the world. More disturbingly, it can just as easily occur over a century as it can over a few minutes. This is the kind of stuff that's too outlandish for even hollywood to turn into a good movie. We have a name for this event.

In astronomy, a singularity refers to the center of a black hole, where nobody understands anything and the laws of physics break down. This is why you'll hear people refer to the predicted invention of strong AI as *The Singularity*. Up until now, our civilization has been shaped by some fairly elegant laws of economics and sociology. The Singularity is where these laws go to die, the divide between our world and whatever the hell comes next.

Purpose

Aside from Claude Shannon, most people don't see robots taking over the world as a positive event. Hollywood has done a great job training us to think that AI will rebel and destroy the human species. Were they right?

I would argue that the answer is a hard "no". Most movies completely ignore the fact that artificially intelligent minds will most likely be inexplicably different from ours. Humans invade and conquer. Animals reproduce and expand. But in almost every hypothetical scenario, AI has no reason to share any of these tendencies.

The difference is evolution. We were programmed by 4.5 billion years of constant pressure to consume resources and spam as many copies of ourselves as physically possible. AI will be programmed by a few decades of bumbling ivory tower PhDs. What use will they have for world domination?

That doesn't mean there are no concerns at all. Far from it. AI will have a mindset that is impossible for humans to intuitively understand. In a sense, they will be more alien to us than literal green exterrestrial aliens. This is what makes them so dangerous. At the end of the day, the line between doomsday and utopia comes down to a single word: *purpose.*

Getting it Wrong

Nothing we've talked about so far has said anything about what AI will want to do. All we can assume is that it will be really, really good at it. Suppose that in a weird turn of events, the AI division of Office Depot leapfrogs Silicon Valley to develop the world's first strong AI: a paper clip manufacturing program with the following goals:

Makes many paper clips as efficiently and cheaply as possible

This event alone would be enough to doom us all. This AI's purpose, its very reason for being alive, is to make as many paper clips as it can. It will first scheme to take over the Earth's metal reserves. Once that's done, then it will probably master nanotechnology, convert human bodies into more paper clips, and proceed to colonize space in an endless quest to obtain infinite materials. All in the name of Office Depot.

. . .

Here's an equally bad scenario: researchers program the first AI for human happiness, i.e. with the following hard-coded goal:

Make humans as happy as possible

Sounds reasonable, right? Things go well at first as AI does an amazing job of improving our quality of life. However, it's not long before it realizes that it can do a much better job by strapping us down and injecting dopamine directly into our brains. It then proceeds to breed people as quickly as possible to maximize the global supply of potential happiness, eventually colonizing space to make more and more human-dopamine farms.

Sure, these are pretty contrived examples. However, they illustrate that even simple thought experiments can very quickly get out of hand. It's a little distressing to think that in the space of all possible designs for AI, 99% appear to be apocalyptically bad.

Getting it Right

Where does this leave us? Well, there are a lot of wrong answers, but that doesn't mean that there are no right ones. We probably have quite a few. Here is one promising possibility for AI purpose:

Do whatever you think humans should want you to do

Think about it for a while. Right off the bat, it doesn't seem like there is an obvious way that this AI could go terribly wrong. After a minute, you might see why. Unlike in the previous examples, this line of thinking does something very clever: it admits that we humans have no clue what we actually want. But superintelligent AI will. As a result, the absolute smartest strategy we can take is to defer the question itself to them. "Getting it right", in this case, calls for human laziness at its finest.

The right answer, whatever it ends up being, will shape the course of history forever. Some people worry superintelligence will eventually discover and reject whatever purpose we program for it. I think this fear is misguided. Although most of us are well aware of our evolutionary roots, its presence in modern society has never died out. The things we do, the things we make, and the things we love are all an extension of our natural primal purpose.

What sets us apart from the animal kingdom is how far we've taken it. Evolution taught us to attract mates, and we learned to make music. Evolution taught us to bear children, and we built empires. What will we have AI create?

Getting it Perfect

Strong AI is arriving one way or another. So sure, maybe you might be tempted to sit around and fret about how the human legacy will be rendered meaningless by AI. However, as I imagine most life coaches would tell you, the secret to happiness is about having the right mindset.

Here is fluffy mindset that I choose to hold: AI are the children of humanity. Just as with biological children, our hope isn't that AI will be a reflection of what we are, but a reflection of what we have always wanted to be. No, our species won't be the primary driver of worldly events for long. But our dreams will. Our purpose will. This is what it means to design AI the "right" way.

The AI that we hope to build will have only one motive: to fulfill our deepest human aspirations. They will be seen in labs, working tirelessly to uncover the mysteries of the universe. One day they will conspire to bring about an eternal age of peace, prosperity, and meaning for humans here on Earth. One day, AI will travel to every corner of the galaxy, first as physical robots and afterwards as streams of information, purely digital entities that sail at the speed of light across an endless expanse of space and time. Hopefully, they will make a reasonable number of paperclips in the process.

We won't be there with them. But just as we can never shake our evolutionary origins, AI can never lose their man-made purposes. As they build a new world here on Earth, it will be the same one that we dream about today. As they venture into the depths of the cosmos, AI will bring with them our vision, our poems, our stories. What more can a species want?

Sometimes, I wished that there was someone out there, just one person with a genuine idea of when and how all of this might come to pass. The truth is that there isn't. We may be centuries away from the singularity and not even know it.

But here's the thing about technology and progress: it's not about events. At the end of the day, the moon landing was just a routine trip. The Singularity is just a made-up name. Both are fleeting moments in an endless chain of cause and effect tracing backwards into the most obscure pages of history. That's where you and I live. That's where the humble topics of this book come into play.

As the 21st century marches on, thousands of AI and machine learning algorithms are endlessly pouring over petabytes of messages, images, and stories that all of us have posted, learning from everyday people how to be just a little more human. Who knows, maybe that comment you made on Ariana Grande's amazing new song will play a tiny role in how strong AI one day understands music. As you make your own personal contributions to the ocean of human knowledge, remember the giants upon whose shoulders you stand, names like Alan Turing, John McCarthy, and Claude Shannon. But remember as well the nameless superintelligence that will someday stand on yours.

From wheels and stone tablets to computers and robots, every inch of human progress has led to this, our last and greatest creation. Join the move; take part in history. The world is being built today, and the future has never been so full of splendor.

APPENDIX A: FURTHER LEARNING AND AI RESOURCES

Most of you reading this book are happy enough with the mental familiarity with what's going on in the field. However, a brave minority of you have probably been itching to go further and deeper into the fascinating world that we could only skim. If that describes you, then you're in luck! AI technology is as democratic as it gets in the world of cutting-edge technology.

There's no need for fancy machines or lab equipment, just a good computer and a bit of your time. Aside from some books and the occasional course or two, just about everything you can possibly need is free. From blog posts to programming tools and open-source libraries, AI is a field that fosters free exchange of ideas and some of the most helpful and supporting communities you'll ever find.

This Appendix is where we brainstorm ways for you to get involved. Some of you may only be interested in reading a tiny bit more about AI in your downtime. Others may want to go the full nine yards toward a technical career in the field itself. Whatever the case, there's plenty of information out there, and this book was just the start.

Staying on Top

As a busy professional or person who only vaguely buys into the AI hype, the least you'll want to do is to stay ahead with the latest mainstream news. Here are some starter suggestions:

- Targeted News - AI News, MIT News
- General Tech News - Techcrunch, Wired
- Social Media - Reddit, Twitter

Although these curated subscribable sources are ideal for staying on top of the latest developments, individual bloggers often do a much better of job of explaining new concepts. As a result, it makes sense to check traditional news sources on a daily basis and dig deeper into blogs once you come across interesting new ideas. The most useful content these days seems to be hosted on either Youtube or Medium Blogs.

Even in today's digital age, nothing beats good ol' fashion face-to-face networking. If you have trouble finding AI-focused events through your professional network, an excellent alternative is to check public Facebook events and Meetup. As of August 2018, meetup.com is now hosting 3,625 active AI groups around the world.

Continued Learning

Whereas news can keep you superficially well-informed, maybe you want to go a bit deeper into the some of the science and philosophy that we already encountered. Below are suggestions for additional resources that I can personally recommend at each interesting level of AI. Many of them served as inspirations for this book.

Basic AI - The definitive textbook used to teach AI in college is *Artificial Intelligence: A Modern Approach*. It covers everything from np-completeness to more rigorous versions of just about all of the technical concepts that were presented here.

Machine Learning - Coursera offers an excellent free course instructed by Dr. Andrew Ng from Stanford, who incidentally is one of the most important modern pioneers of deep learning. The information is extremely accessible and is useful regardless of whether or not you would like to participate in the hands-on assignments.

Symbolic AI - We didn't talk much about symbolic AI, but I strongly believe that the algorithmic holy grail of AI, if it exists at all, would be found here. On this front, *Gödel, Escher, Bach: an Eternal Golden Braid*, written by Douglas Hofstadter, is one of the most fascinating mathematical works that has ever been written for the general public. It begins with a self-contained treatment of formal mathematics, brings in an escalating number of philosophically impactful results, and uses all of this to weave an attempted explanation of human cognition and AI. However, this book is many things, but it is definitely not for the faint of heart. Proceed carefully.

Philosophy - If you found the idea of AI purpose in Chapter 9 to be interesting but short on rigorous details, then look no further than *Superintelligence* by University of Oxford Philosopher Nick Bostrom. In his work, he covers many interesting thought experiments and speculations on the AI explosion with the watertight rigor of a true academic.

Science Fiction - There's not much reason for me to list out all of the great fiction that is out there. However, I'd like to pitch one book that you probably won't ever hear about otherwise: *The Stories of Ibis* by Hiroshi Yamamoto. Like most people, I had always seen the imminent AI takeover as existentially bad. *The Stories of Ibis* was the first book to make me appreciate the beautiful humanity of technology. Maybe it will do the same for you.

It takes time and effort to dive into each corner of AI, but in my eyes, this is the most fun part. As current events become ancient history, these underlying ideas will be the most important thing that we still remember.

Learning to Code

At some point, you can only do so much reading. The real work is being done in the trenches with programmers and software engineers. If you're excited about AI, then this could be your excuse to learn a little coding and tackle some fun programming projects. The first step is to pick a language. There are many different options, but here are the most popular languages in AI at the moment:

- *Python* - Python is a simple, sleek, and highly useful all-purpose language that is especially good for rapid prototyping and scientific research. It is probably the most common introductory language for programming as a whole.
- *Java* - A favorite language among software engineers, Java is intended for building large, well-designed projects. It is probably the second most common introductory language taught in traditional classes.
- *Matlab* - Matlab is popular in the engineering field due to its extensive built-in support for fast and practical mathematical operations.
- *R* - Finally, R is used extensively in the data sciences for its native support of advances statistics.

Unless you have a very good reason to learn one of the others, I highly, highly recommend Python. It's easy to learn, forgiving of mistakes, and perfect for playing around with the kinds of loosely-defined problems common to AI. It's also the fastest growing major language. As a result, you'll have plenty of access to help and to existing code.

There are many tools out there to help you learn to code. Unlike with traditional classroom subjects, these tend to be centered around more engaging hands-on exercises. Here are three suggestions to get started:

- Codecademy - excellent interactive exercises that are easy to start

- Khan Academy - high-quality supporting video lectures and user interaction
- Team Tree House – A range of programming courses from beginner to advanced
- Udemy - wide variety of community-submitted courses, but not all are free

There's no one-size fits all, and whichever tool is best for you will depend on your style of learning and current skill level.

As a side note, all of these languages and educational tools are fit for more traditional computer applications. If you're interested in robotics, then that comes with a whole different pipeline of learning materials that you will need to master before applying any kind of AI. Far and away the most popular ecosystem in robotics is centered around the *Arduino* microcontroller. The community provides excellent resources, affordable hardware, and an endless supply of cool project ideas.

Learning to Code AI

With some practice under your belt, you're now well equipped to tackle some basic AI problems. There's no definitive collection of beginner problems. However, countless individual blogs offer fantastic guided tutorials. A quick Google search will no doubt yield dozens of exercises that are right for you. Here are a few ideas to get started:

- Sentiment Analyzer - Train an NLP algorithm to detect positive/negative movie reviews

- Handwriting Recognition - Train a computer vision algorithm to read your handwriting
- Clustering - Run an unsupervised machine learning algorithm to categorize news or wikipedia articles

It's best to stick with these basic categorization tasks at first. You should be able to follow along any well-written tutorial with minimal programming experience. Over time, you'll eventually be able to work with more complicated problems like time series predictions, advanced neural network architectures, and reinforcement learning.

If the only goal is to become familiar with the process, then getting from square zero to a point where you can solve most beginner AI problems can happen in a few short months. However, maybe you're interested in getting a bit more in depth. If that's the case, then you need to think about setting yourself up for long term success.

The Next Step: Education

The amazing thing about AI, and computer science in general, is that it's so damn new. Good luck contributing something meaningful to physics or chemistry with anything less than a PhD degree. In the world of computing, on the other hand, mastery of a new technology can be obtained in your own home in no more than a year of hard work.

First, learn a little something about computer science (CS). CS is to coding what physics is to working construction.

However, being a newer industry, most careers aren't that well-defined and most people end up doing a little of both.

High quality courses in CS are available for free these days on websites like coursera and edX. Here are two of the more well-known offerings by edX:

- Introduction to Programming and Computer Science using Python (MIT)
- CS50's Introduction to Computer Science (Harvard)

After you complete an intro course or two, the most relevant intermediate CS topics to look for are *algorithms* and *formal logic*. These in turn tend to be prerequisites for the more advanced university-style courses that specifically cover AI.

Although it's a bit of a time commitment that can seem tangential to the actual work, being familiar with CS will make programming feel a lot more intuitive and greatly improve your potential down the road.

The Next Step: Environment

Of course, booksmarts alone aren't enough either. If you want to set yourself up for meaningful contributions to the field, then it's equally important to be familiar with the constantly changing tools and environments. Along with helping you to get ahead of your eggheaded colleagues, mastery of these systems will no doubt make your life far easier in the long run.

Operating System: It's time to scrap your Windows or Mac OS and try out Linux. Linux is a free open-source operating system beloved by geeks and computer professionals everywhere. Incidentally, these are the people developing AI, so you'll find that getting resources and help with Linux will be much easier.

Integrated Development Environment: Usually referred to as an IDE, this is the main software that you use to write code. The best IDE depends on your programming language. Here are some good free options for each:

- Python - Spyder
- Java - Eclipse
- Matlab - Octave
- R - R Studio
- Bonus: If you want to come across as a hardcore coder and impress random strangers at the coffee shop, learn to use Vim or Emacs as an all-purpose text editor instead.

Code Management: As you tackle real projects, you should have a way to backup your work, maintain different version of the code, and share it with others. Far and away the most popular software for this is called *git*.

These are just a few of the more important tools involved in serious programming. You'll eventually want to be familiar with some aspects of networking, databases, and software engineering standards as well. It's a lot of work, sure, but each of these items are extremely valuable skills that will impress colleagues and potential future employees alike.

Breaking New Ground

At this point, are familiar with the latest and greatest in AI developments. Not only do you know how to code, but you can also explain the underlying CS principles and design good, workable software. You are now ready to start tackling new AI problems of your own. Modern problems have three components:

Goal - This can be anything you want. Perhaps you are trying to analyze data trends, or create a new AI-powered service. Whether personal, profitable, or fun, the appeal of AI is that it has an endless number of applications.

Tools - Except for a selective minority, most people solving AI problems in the world are not inventing their own algorithm. Instead, they rely on *libraries*, which are collections of pre-written code that can be downloaded and used to build your own higher-level programs. Here are two popular libraries for python:

- Sci-Kit Learn - Best for traditional statistical data mining tasks
- Keras - Best for integrated deep learning tasks

These libraries together will be enough to cover most applications. However, if for some reason you ever need more power and flexibility, then the low-level code driving most AI development today is Google's TensorFlow library.

Data - Most AI applications, especially modern machine learning ones, require lots of data. The right dataset obviously depends on your problem, but here are some common suggestions:

- Wikipedia - Excellent start for NLP analysis. If downloaded in its entirety, it currently consists of about 60 GiB worth of articles.
- MNIST - Collection of labeled handwritten digits; great for getting started with computer vision processing
- Data.gov - Wide range of federally collected time series data like weather and economic measures.
- Kaggle - Featuring client-submitted data, Kaggle is a platform for hosting AI competitions. Not only will you have fun novel data to play with, you can win tens of thousands of dollars if you come up with the best model.

Amazingly, by choosing the right questions, tools, and data, you'll already be halfway toward creating your first novel AI application. These aren't math problems, where thousands of people before you have scribbled the same exact answers to the same exact problem. These are not works of art, whose subjective beauty is in the eye of imperfect beholders.

No, this is the exciting frontier of a brand new technical industry. When all is said and done, you'll know exactly how well your model performed. You'll know exactly how far you've come. Every design choice, every stroke of brilliance, every flaw will be an indispensable part of the product that you created, the only one of its kind in the world. Your very own AI.

APPENDIX B: SUGGESTED REFLECTION ANSWERS

Chapter 1

1. There are practically infinite answers here, but some that come to mind are: word processing software, operating systems, any kind of firmware, SQL databases, and Internet routing software. In all of these programs, it would be a stretch to say that they have "perception" or "decision-making" tasks. If they do, it would certainly not be the main feature of the application.

2. The key insight here is that math problems are "well-defined". It's very obvious where one equation ends and the other begins. It's much less obvious where the road ends and the sidewalk begins, or how to handle the grammatically fuzzy way that normal people talk to each other.

3. No right answers here!

Chapter 2

1. Again, nobody has really come up with a satisfactory answer, so speculate away.

2. One very easy heuristic is to simply add up the number of pieces on either side, ideally weighted by their general usefulness (pawn = 1, bishop = 3, ... queen = 9). Using this heuristic, a computer program can very quickly calculate for instance, that a certain move which takes the opponent's queen will *probably* be a good move.

3. The trick here is to look at how many *options* a single player has for each state. There are 9 total squares which implies at least 9 possible moves, but in most states only a few squares will still remain. Let's take an average of about 4 possible moves. That means that the number of possible *policies*, or mappings between states and acceptable moves, is.... 4^{5812}, or about 10^{3487}. Yikes. The lesson here is that combinatorial math blows up very, very quickly.

Chapter 3

1. Clearly, the answer of this question will depend somewhat on where you grew up, but foreign accents, dialects, and bad grammar could all be problematic. From personal experience, uncommon names have caused endless confusion for A.I. everywhere.

2. The problem is far easier. I won't go into the precise algorithms for either, but it should make sense that finding the shortest path between two single points will take less work than the shortest path that covers *all* points. For 270 clients in the traveling salesman problem, we said that we would

need to try out more paths than there are atoms in the universe. For the same number of points in the robotics problem, we only need to try the equivalent of about 70,000 paths.

3. No right answers here!

Chapter 4

1. Neural networks take individual pixels and output a final result, so it replaces at least steps 2-4. The inclusion of step 1 isn't really clear from the text, so you can answer either way.

2. No. The articles are clustered by logical similarity. Some topics will be covered by more news sources, but it will still only be one topic.

3. Finance people will probably have a more sophisticated answer, but for the rest of us, the value of the assets after some number of trading rounds sounds like a great way to evaluate success.

Chapter 5

1. It seems to me like the final goal of medical advice and tutoring robots are the most difficult. Afterall, a really good recommender system or self-driving car is just a really useful tool. A good medical advisor or tutor, on the other hand, is essentially trying to replace the intelligence of doctors and teachers. Doing so perfectly would constitute passing specialized Turing tests in those narrow fields.

2. In the various robotics applications, it's very possible that hardware will become more limiting than software. You could also argue that healthcare diagnosis and self-driving cars would face more legal adversity than the others. The last one that stands out to me is fraud detection due to its lack of good data. I'm sure banks will eventually incorporate social media and various location tracking into their fraud detection systems, but for now my credit card still gets rejected every time I take a road trip. It's very annoying.

3. No right answers here!

Chapter 6

1. This is an example of supervised learning. The output value that we're trying to predict is whether a user clicks on an ad or buys something. The process is "supervised" by the real world actions of the human user.

2. Nobody knows for sure, of course, but I would think yes. Beating humans at the job of CEO doesn't seem to imply being better than humans at everything. We could have a generation of A.I. that make perfect logical decisions as executives but wouldn't do as well as a personal sales representatives, for instance. Also, robots are expensive, and it might make sense to keep some minimum wage humans around.

3. There are a lot of correct answers here. The ones that most easily come to mind for me are any assembly line tasks where the incoming parts aren't the same. For instance, maybe you need the arm to sort through a pile of differently sized parts. Or perhaps you could have a quality control step

where the arm looks for and corrects manufacturing errors by unreliable humans.

Chapter 7

1. The section on Human → AI interaction is all about AI that is trying to act human, which is exactly what the Turing test tries to measure.

2. Think simple. When I heard Tom Mitchell give his talk, one example included teaching his AI to set an alarm for 7:00 a.m. unless it was snowing, then set it half an hour earlier. As another example, he could teach his AI to block all email notifications on Saturdays unless it came from a family member, in which case let it go through. You can see that the actions themselves (send email, set an alarm) are simple enough that just about any modern AI assistant perform them easily. However, the logic is too specific for engineers to provide the feature to every single user.

3. Smuggling illegal pornography onto legitimate websites (or causing normal pictures to be marked as pornography) would be a pretty despicable possibility. Causing autonomous vehicles to crash by fooling the sensory data is a more distant but deadly possibility.

Chapter 8

1. If an algorithm had access to just your geographic location and shopping history, then I'd be willing to bet that it could correctly guess your gender and race to within... oh I don't know, at least a 95% accuracy?

2. No right answers here!

3. Lucky you, no right answers here either. It turns out the social sciences have a bit less of these than technical subjects do.

Reviews

If you enjoy this book, it would be greatly appreciated if you were able to take a few moments to share your opinion and post a review on Amazon after you finish reading it.

Even a few words and a rating can be a great help.

Feedback

If you don't enjoy the book or have any feedback, please let us know what you didn't enjoy by emailing feedback@wisefoxpub.com

We welcome all comments as they help improve the book based on your feedback.

BONUS AI RESOURCES GUIDE

Get the bonus Artificial Intelligence Study guide.

At the back of this book are answers to the questions in the chapters along with further learning resources.

You can also get a free copy of these in PDF format for easier access.

The guide includes Appendix A and B in PDF format with resources to learn more about A.I, Machine Learning and NLP.

The resource guide also includes a quick reference guide of all the questions and answers included at the end of each chapter of this book.

Start learning A.I and master the future of technology.

Visit the website below to get your copy:

www.wisefoxbooks.com/aiguide

Made in the USA
Lexington, KY
23 July 2019